REDEEMED!

REDEEMED!

HOW I SURVIVED ADDICTION, A SUICIDE ATTEMPT, AND DIVORCE TO FIND MY WAY BACK TO THE CROSS

MICHAEL STEIMEL

ISBN: 978-1-7379244-5-6

Publishing services provided by Fitting Words LLC
Cover design by LACreative
Front cover photos and permissions from iStock (church photo) and Shutterstock (cross photo).
Back cover author photo from Michael Steimel
Page layout by Win-Win Words LLC

Printed in the United States of America

This book is dedicated to the "least of these."

"And the King will say, I tell you the truth, when you did it to one of the least of these, you were doing it to me."
— Matt. 25:40

Contents

Introduction

My name is Michael and I am an alcoholic. If that sounds like one of those canned introductions you hear at a twelve-step Alcoholics Anonymous (AA) meeting, it is because that's exactly what it is. Not only am I an alcoholic, but I am an alcoholic born again from a sinful past and am now eighteen years sober. I am also a self-employed businessman in a potentially lucrative field of work that has allowed me to work in or at least drive through nearly all fifty states in the good ol' US of A.

For the past thirty-plus years I have crisscrossed the country assembling, erecting, and climbing giant cell phone towers reaching hundreds of feet into the sky and scattered across the countryside. Maybe you've spotted some of them while motoring by on an interstate highway or lonely country road. They are quite a sight to see, almost like something out of a science fiction movie in which alien spaceships attack Earth.

The tower business can be a dangerous occupation—fall and you're probably dead within seconds. But it's a profitable one, even lucrative at times, provided you know how to manage money and live a responsible life of common sense and frugality. Those happen to be two qualities that were alien to me, which was my fault, for more than half my life. Being a town drunk from the time you are in your early teens can do that to a man (or woman).

I once read where divorce, alcohol rehab, and bankruptcy are three of the most stressful things a person can go through in his or her life. I'll vouch for that. But try going through all three at once. I did and it was anything but fun—it was horrendous; three destructive forces pulling at me all at once. My lesson of the day today is to not try this at home. We all know that fat, drunk, and stupid is no way to go through life, son; neither is being divorced, drunk, and destitute.

It doesn't get much worse than this: at age thirty-three, lying on a bed upstairs at home, I pulled out my .38-caliber pistol, loaded a round into the chamber, stuck the barrel in my mouth, and pulled the trigger. Blood and guts everywhere. It looked like a hand grenade had been detonated inside my mouth. But I was still alive, still conscious, and still aware of what I had just tried to do. I was now in a state of shock, accompanied by the intense level of physical pain that can bring a man to his knees, especially one with a self-inflicted bullet lodged somewhere in his head.

There also was the time I spent a week locked up in a mental ward, eating (actually, sipping) exclusively broth while sleeping 95 percent of the time. I knew that if I ever wanted a normal life for myself and my daughters, Courtney and Grace, then four and two, respectively, that things would have to change. Their mother—my ex—wasn't much help, which I will discuss later in this book. After discussing my condition (robust alcoholism mixed with the pain of a botched suicide attempt) with my parents and my older brother Steve (I also have a younger brother, Tony), I decided I would go to rehab. That meant a trip to Miami Beach, Florida, and a rehab facility that family members had found for me.

Steve drove me from Indianapolis to Miami. I must have been quite the sight (bystanders seeing me must have thought Halloween had come early), my nose and face heavily bandaged, and both sides of my face—my cheeks—black from the impact of the bullet. I remember thinking about the road that lay ahead for me, not just rehabbing from a bullet to my head but in my ongoing battle with the bottle and a nasty divorce linked to custody wars with my ex-wife and the fates and health of our two daughters.

My life started turning for the better when my mother bought me a recovery Bible, and it went with me everywhere I went. For the first time in my life, I started reading and studying the Bible. I still have that same one today. I spent a few weeks in rehab in Miami, then flew home to Indiana to start rebuilding my life. The phone calls, letters, and cards I received were in the hundreds. I thought I had no friends, but found out different through those difficult circumstances. Of course, all my drinking friends disappeared like cockroaches in the woodwork once I quit drinking. I had alcohol withdrawals for over a year, and I suffered many anxiety attacks. All I could do each time was just lie there and shake until it passed over. I also suffered from head trauma, and there would be times I would have a breakdown for no reason and without warning. This went on for more than three years.

Okay, I'm getting too deep into the book's narrative, and I don't want to spoil the rest of my story. You'll have to keep turning the pages for the rest of it. What I hope you will get out of this book is how redemption and restoration can change anyone's life for the better. It doesn't matter where you are in your own life and no matter how bad, discouraged, or hopeless you might feel. I found a way out of it through prayer, Scripture, church fellowship, and a committed relationship with Jesus Christ, my Savior. For much of the last twenty years, I have had the opportunity to speak dozens of times to church groups, school assemblies, and prison inmates, among others, about my life, all while giving my testimony and baring my soul in front of others. My thought is that maybe I am throwing them a life preserver they can grab onto, so they can keep their heads above water and eventually be set free from the sort of trappings that almost derailed and buried me almost two decades ago.

I owe my life to God, my family, and too many others to mention. Thank you for allowing me to share my story.

May God bless you!!

REDEEMED!

1
Fool on the Hill

ALCOHOL CAN BE A KILLER. It doesn't take cirrhosis of the liver, an extreme case of alcohol poisoning, or being drunk behind the steering wheel of a moving vehicle to prove that. I know this firsthand. Mix a wrecked marriage, financial stress amid a looming bankruptcy, and a heaping helping of despair, despondency, and depression together. Then place your hand on the trigger of a loaded .38, and you have the cocktail recipe for a quick trip to the afterlife. I know; I was there.

From the time I was a young boy, barely a teen, I was a drunk. I didn't know I was an alcoholic at the time, but chalk that up to youthful denial. I wasn't the proverbial town drunk growing up sloshed every night in Sullivan, a town in southwestern Indiana, but I drank way more than your typical hard-partying high school student. It was a way of life that followed me into my twenties and my thirties, and it didn't stop after I got married—it only got worse. My wife and I were both problem drinkers. It became an even bigger problem between us and ate away at whatever sanity there might have ever been in our relationship.

It was thought by many—including my parents and, of course, me—that I had psychological issues during my youth, not necessarily related to my drinking. Nothing to really put your finger on or give a name to if you lack understanding of mental illness. Depression combined with anxiety, maybe? Drinking alcohol, whether consistently in excess by some (e.g., me and one of my brothers) or in relative moderation (pretty much everyone else in my family), was so common where I grew up that it wasn't even considered a problem. No matter, I still believe alcohol was the root of everything negative in my life. I remember lying in bed with my wife on many occasions, telling her that my main problem was alcohol and that it would someday kill me.

After a few years of fighting my drinking, my wife gave in and joined me. Now both of us were drinking every night, and that caused even more craziness in our lives. With the money we were making from my erecting telephone towers through our company, we lived it up fairly well. This was in the late 1990s and into the early 2000s, when cellular telephone service was really taking off and signal towers were popping up as abundantly as daisies in fields across America. I had already been in the business for nearly a decade, starting not long after (barely) graduating from high school. If you knew what you were doing, which I did most of the time—despite all the drinking—you could make good money.

On my then-wife Joanna's birthday, we would rent a limousine and have big parties. One year we put on a dance with a band at the local American Legion hall. At different times we hosted parties at our farm with a deejay and kegs of beer. It wasn't long before we were spending a lot of time—too much time, it turns out—hanging out at the taverns and clubs. Against an agreement we had made back when we had gotten married, we would even go out drinking separately. Much of the time we didn't even wait for sundown before we would head out to hit the hot spots, of which there weren't many in our neck of woods. As long as the beer was cold and the music good enough to dance to, though, who cared? We would take the girls to daycare, and have the rest of the day to ourselves. There was a point when we were making more money and working less. Many times we would sit in the tavern all afternoon, and then go pick up the girls from daycare and head home. There were several nights we would put the girls in car seats and drive around drinking till late at night. Eventually, that irresponsible lifestyle would be our ruin.

You're Fired!

One morning in June 2001, I decided to fire all our employees. There was no prior planning, nor consideration given to the ramifications. It was purely on impulse. At the time we had several good job contracts waiting for us and an already thriving business. Then I go and screw things up by handing out pink slips en masse—I fired everyone else on the spot. I just didn't care anymore. I was very unhappy and miserable with my life, no doubt feeling sorry for myself.

It wasn't long before our income started dwindling down to next to nothing. Two things struck me about our impending predicament and trip to hell: First, it never ceased to amaze me how two individuals could burn through such large gobs of money in the short amount of time we did; and second, even with most of our money dried up, we somehow managed to find the logic to keep on partying as much as ever.

About six months into this whirlwind experience of living it up while watching ourselves in deep water circling the proverbial bathtub drain, we decided to have an auction and try to liquidate a lot of our assets and then save what we could cobble together in terms of cash. Cash is king, right? (As long as you know what to do with it.) We managed to sell all of our company's equipment, some farm equipment, and one of our other nearby properties for which I had plunked down wads of cash without any real thought as to why I was doing it. In hindsight, I must have been playing some high-stakes game of real-life Monopoly, believing that the more acres I owned, the better off we would be for our future. If there had been a Boardwalk or Park Place in our vicinity, I probably would have bought them, too. What I once held in spending money, I lacked in common sense and purpose.

The result was good—we netted some money to keep us going for a while, but it didn't help our income problem. We had no cash flow coming in because our company was essentially at a standstill. We started getting behind on our financial obligations, such as mortgage payments and the installments on equipment we had purchased. The bank was applying pressure and eventually started foreclosure proceedings on our farm and properties. Our response: we drank even more, and our marriage continued on a downhill spiral.

Throughout 2002 our lives were in turmoil, with our bad behaviors exacerbated by the fact that by then we had two very young daughters—Courtney, born in 1998, and Grace in 2000. Welcome to our fallen world, girls. As for Joanna and me, our lives consisted of more drinking, more arguing, and more holes in the walls. There were times when she would have a temporary breakdown, and I believe I was in a constant state of breakdown.

First Came the Bankruptcy

That fall, we sobered up long enough to consult an attorney and file Chapter 13 bankruptcy in an effort to save our home. We knew we couldn't pay the payments, and bankruptcy was just a way of prolonging our shared descent. With our company now officially kaput, and little other choice for me, I started doing some contract work for my brother's company. That was all in an effort to feed my family, and with any luck, keep that roof over our heads. Because of my job—I was still involved in putting up cell towers—I was gone traveling a lot, and that put more stress on our failing marriage.

We made it through Christmas that year without major incident and without losing the home (yet). Then I went back to traveling on business after New Year's. It might have been a new year, but everything was getting old for me quickly in early 2003. I was in terrible physical pain from all the booze and searing mental anguish from all the financial and marital stresses. I had been sent on a job to Minneapolis, Minnesota, a ten-hour drive from home that felt more like twenty. I was by myself the whole way, giving me plenty of uninterrupted time to do a lot of thinking about the hell my life had become. I cried a lot, sobbing at times, wiping my eyes as needed so I could see the endless road in front of me, knowing that things were in shambles. I was in so much pain, I did something that I never thought I would do. I cried out, "God, I know I gave up on you years ago and said I didn't need you, but God I need you now! God, I can't live this way anymore. If you still love me, show me the way."

Little did I know at the time that God had heard my prayer, but his answer was still a ways away. Soon, my life would be turned upside down; things got worse before they could get better. Easy to say in hindsight. I spoke that prayer on a Wednesday and got back home that Saturday. That night, my wife and I went out to a local club and we danced what turned out to be our last dance, seventeen years after we had danced our first as immature teenagers. I can still hear the band, at my request, playing "Wonderful Tonight." We didn't go home together, and we never spent another night with each other after that. The next day we separated—she going to stay with friends and I still living back at home with the girls, who were now two and four. That was my first day of thousands to come in my new role as Mr. Mom, although it soon became clear I was not in it for the long haul, at least not in my sickened mind.

Then Came Divorce

After a few days of Joanna being gone, I decided to file for divorce. In retaliation, she put a restraining order on me. Nice. There you have it—love and marriage. I really believed that if we could just talk face to face, we could settle it between us, but she wasn't talking. She flat refused.

On the day we went to our first court hearing, the local judge refused to hear our case because he knew me and my family, so he recused himself. The judge wasn't alone; most people in the county knew my family. The hearing ended up being postponed for another month or so, and it was ultimately held in a neighboring county. The battle raged on, and all our so-called friends took sides. Our attorneys agreed on letting her see the kids during the day. I would drop them off at daycare in the morning, and she would pick them up and drop them off back there at about four in the afternoon. Then I would take them home for the evening.

My wife and I were both still drinking and not speaking to each other. I was trying to work, raise the girls, and deal with the stress of our bankruptcy, and I managed to keep up with my drinking. I sent her a few notes begging her to speak with me and work things out. Finally, she relented and agreed to talk with me. But it never happened. I waited at the house, but she never showed up. Eventually I called her, only for her to tell me that she wasn't going to talk with me. I hung up the phone and immediately started shaking. Soon I was sweating, experiencing chest pains, and unable to catch my breath. It felt like a heart attack. I was able to call my mother, and she quickly came over and took me to the hospital emergency room, where they checked me out and told me I was having an anxiety attack. I had never experienced one before and didn't know what it was, but for a while there I was thinking the worst, wondering if I was about to die.

As the hospital staff was getting ready to discharge me from the ER, they asked me if I was suicidal. By then I knew I pretty much was, but after having already spent many nights in stress wards (more on that later), I knew if I said yes they would keep me there, and I wanted out. So, I answered, "No, I'm not suicidal." They gave me a bottle of Xanax, after which my mother took me home.

Looking back, I had lived much of my life as though I had a death wish. Toward that end, alcohol was almost my constant companion. One of my alcohol-induced joys was riding ATVs at seventy miles per hour down a gravel road, drunk, no helmet. What do you call that? Then there were the pills, which are tiny and don't look like much, but handled improperly they can kill even a big guy like me, six-foot-four and over two hundred pounds, without much problem, perhaps slowly.

On one occasion, I had been drinking all day, when I got into an argument with my parents and my wife. It got so bad that I got it within me that I would kill myself with a bottle full of painkillers—Vicodin. That put me in the hospital, where they pumped out my stomach and I eventually finished vomiting. My parents were there, as was my wife. Once my stomach had been pumped, I said, "Okay, I'm ready to go." But the doctors said, "No, you're not going anywhere. You can't. You tried to hurt yourself, and we've got the right to keep you."

So they put me in the mental ward on one of the hospital's upper floors. I stayed for about a week, during which the doctors came to check on me every day. I went to group therapy and saw a counselor. I think that was the first time I had been put on any medication, after which they added an antidepressant. After going home, I stayed sober for a few weeks and even went to church a couple of times. Things were good. I wasn't drinking, my wife wasn't drinking, and things seemed a lot better in our lives. It wasn't long, though, before I started drinking again. I was an alcoholic.

I had started seeing a counselor for a couple of months before I overdosed on those Vicodin pills. After leaving the hospital that time, I started going once a month to see the same psychiatrist in order to get refills of the antidepressants I had been prescribed, and I was a different person—a better person—on the antidepressants, even with my drinking. But I wouldn't always take them. I would do really well for a few months then I would quit taking them and be right back where I started. Then I'd take them again.

Even though I was working with a male psychiatrist and a husband-and-wife psychologist team, I never told them about my drinking. I knew if I did that, they would diagnose me as an alcoholic. Then I would have to answer to my wife and everyone else who knew me. The husband-and-wife team eventually moved out of town to another county, so I found another psychologist to see periodically. While I liked him a lot, I didn't tell him about my drinking either. Again, I was feeling better. What I would talk to him about was business stuff and how to handle certain things that came up on the job, such as stressors. The medication kept me leveled out even with all the drinking, but it would have helped me more if I had stopped drinking. Taking an antidepressant and drinking a depressant doesn't make a lot of sense. Eventually, I quit going to the psychologist as well as the psychiatrist. On top of that, I later quit taking the medication. My version of *Death Wish*—yet another sequel.

Then there was my playing around with explosives. We had fuel tanks on our property. One was gas and the other was diesel, and they were each stored in three-hundred-gallon fuel tanks. I was always taking gas and pouring it on stuff and lighting it. Sort of a hobby—a sick one. I'd be lighting stuff and blowing it up. Or I would pour gas into a can and shoot it to make it explode. In a similar manner, I would fill a jug with water, put a cap on it, and shoot it with a gun to make the water explode all over the place. It was a thrill a minute, even though no one else seemed impressed.

I'd also burn brush piles. I'd clear out various parts of my property and end up with these big piles of tree limbs and brush, working until late at night. Of course, I was (still) drunk by then, so I would dump gas all over these piles, light them, and watch them burn. Any time I could see something burn was pretty cool. My wife thought I was crazy. She kept her distance most of the time; in fact, she usually didn't even come out of the house when she saw what I was up to in one of those moments. This craziness was still going on with me when the girls were really young, although I'm thankful that neither daughter can remember my drinking. As I write this, it's been eighteen years sober for me—not a drink since.

Then there was the time when I started a fight with members of one of my crews and ended up getting gouged in the eye by one of them. There were four or five guys in that crew who had been working somewhere on the road, and I remember waiting for them when they got back. As soon as they arrived, the crew foreman told me that a couple of them were quitting. By this time, I was already three shades drunk. By now it was nighttime, and when somebody came by in their car to pick them up, I started an argument with one of them and started swinging at him. One of the other guys grabbed me from behind and held my arms, and that's when the guy I had been swinging at came at me and poked his finger in my eye, gouging me, with one guy holding me from behind, although I finally broke loose of that. When they took off running, I ran after them but before I could catch them, they all jumped into a car and were gone, so I never got the chance to retaliate.

As the adrenaline wore off, I realized that my eye was in bad shape, and I couldn't drive because of it. So I called a good friend of mine, and he came by and drove me to the hospital. I had to wait six and a half hours there before someone looked at it, only to tell me there was nothing they could do for me there. So my buddy drove me to the Methodist Hospital in Indianapolis, where an eye specialist looked at it and said I was going to be okay, but that I needed to see a surgeon. So the next day I went back to the hospital and saw the eye surgeon, who ended up making a determination that I didn't need surgery. Instead, he put some eye drops into my eye and then covered it with a patch. It ended up healing by itself, but it took a lot of time before I could see properly out of it again.

Which brings me back to the day after I had the anxiety attack after that brief phone call with my wife, with my mom subsequently taking me to the hospital ER. That's where I got the Xanax and exited the hospital, having told them I was not suicidal. I lied.

The next morning, I took the girls to daycare as usual, and sometime in there I decided that this would be the day to end my life. The emotional pain from the divorce, the stress and disappointment from losing everything, and all the physical pain and sickness from twenty years of alcoholism had finally done me in. I remember thinking, *Age thirty-three, not too bad, actually made it longer than I had planned.*

After dropping off the girls at daycare, I drove along country roads to a town across the state line, where I bought a bottle of Jack Daniel's and a case of beer. I then took my time driving home, a beer in one hand, because I knew this would be my last drive through the country, and I wanted to take it all in. About halfway home, I stopped and vomited, then I resumed driving and continued to drink.

After I got home, I went down to the basement, which wasn't unusual for me—I had spent a ton of time down there. I had an old phonograph of my grandpa's as well as several old albums. I grabbed one of them and stuck it on the turntable and played the Roy Clark song, "Yesterday When I Was Young." I always related well to that song, especially the part that says, ". . . the time has come for me to pay for yesterday, when I was young." I knew that all my problems were a compilation of twenty years of drunkenness, coupled with a sinful life and a refusal to let God in.

As I kept drinking, I decided to take the bottle of Xanax they had given me at the hospital. I might as well be relaxed, right? My mother called sometime that afternoon to check on me, and I told her I was doing fine. She couldn't tell the difference. A couple hours later, my dad called and I told him the same thing—I was fine. At that point, lying was coming easy to me. What my parents didn't know was that earlier in the day I had placed my Smith and Wesson .38 on my bed with plans of using it to end my misery. I was glad my grandfather, whom I talk about more later, wasn't alive to see how my life was ending, especially with that being his gun that was lying on my bed. Sometime during the day, I wrote my final note. Even though I don't remember writing it, it was found in my bedroom and it was in my handwriting. Somehow, through the booze and pills, I had been able to communicate the feelings of a man getting ready to end it all.

This is what the note said:

Please Hear Me Cry
My body aches from the pain,
My baby blues flow like rain,
Please hear me cry.

I go through life as if it were a race,
Don't be fooled by my smiling face,
Please hear me cry.
I'm lost, like a ship at sea,
The man in the mirror just isn't me,
Please hear me cry.
If God sends blessings to those in need,
Then why does my soul continue to bleed?
Please hear me cry.
It has been said, "The Lord first you shall seek,"
I've lost my Lord and I'm growing weak.
Please hear me cry.
In many ways I have been blessed,
With no peace of mind, there is no rest,
Please hear me cry.
I'm tired, I'm weak, I'm ready to die,
As my final request,
Please hear me cry.

I went outside and took one last drunken walk around my farm. It was a cold but sunny February day. As I stumbled around, thoughts raced through my mind of brighter days and happier times, which only made my current state of emotional and physical anguish that much more palpable. I thought about the day we were married, and all the promises that lay ahead. The day we moved into our farm and, of course, our bringing two beautiful angels into the world.

I remember thinking, *It really doesn't matter anymore, and it's all going to be over shortly. This is the life I chose, and the life I lived, and I must accept my destiny*. I felt bad for all the people I had let down, and I cried at the fact that my daughters would never know me. After a while, I headed back into the house, ready to finish the game. It was a game I had played, and one that I had played hard without fear. Now the game was over, and all the players had moved on, with only the loser left on the field. Me.

Once back inside, I shut the door and locked it behind me. I went upstairs and into my room, and laid on the bed, in a shameful voice saying, "God, please forgive me," as I sprawled there.

I had taken the cordless phone with me, and made one final call to my younger brother, Tony, at the office he shared with our older brother, Steve. I don't remember a lot about the conversation, but I do remember thanking him for everything before we hung up. While lying on the bed, I put the .38 caliber revolver in my mouth and, without hesitation, pulled the trigger.

Somehow I stayed conscious as the bullet ripped through the roof of my mouth, lodging itself somewhere in my head. When the gun kicked, it knocked out all my front teeth and split my upper lip and gums. Blood and pieces of flesh were sprayed all over the bed and wall. My mouth was gushing blood, and although I was in shock, I could feel everything. I remember thinking, as my eyes moved around the room, *How is this possible?*

I started thinking about pulling the trigger a second time, but a realization was washing over me that said *I wasn't meant to die*. Instead, I grabbed the cordless phone and again called my brothers' office. Someone there called 911 on my behalf, and soon Tony was headed out to my house (Steve was in Georgia at the time, going through the U.S. Army's Pre-Ranger School at Fort Benning). It was after I hung up the phone that I passed out. I don't know how long I was unconscious before Tony got there, but in that interim I experienced some type of strange visions. I kept hearing my daughters crying out to me, "*Come back, Daddy, come back!*" To this day, I don't know if it was some type of dream, hallucination, or something God was putting into my head, but whatever it was, it was vivid.

When Tony arrived, he kicked in the door and ran upstairs to find me in a pool of blood. When he walked in, he woke me up by saying, "*Why in the hell did you do that?*" He then grabbed the gun to get it away from me. I mumbled a few words, but I didn't have an answer for him.

Before long, a deputy sheriff walked in, and then some members of the local volunteer fire department, followed soon by two EMTs, both of whom I knew personally. One was a young woman I had gone to school with, and the other was a drinking buddy of mine, one of many, in fact. They explained to me that they wouldn't be able to get the gurney up two flights of stairs, so they asked me if I could somehow get up and make it down to the main level of the house. To everyone's amazement, including mine, I was able to get up off the bed and stand up, walk down both sets of stairs, and then lie down on the gurney. They rolled me outside and placed me into the back of the ambulance. Then they started down our long driveway for the trip to the hospital ER, where I had been just about twenty-four hours earlier because of my anxiety attack.

As I was lying there, I could prop up my head just enough to look out the back windows of the ambulance. My dream house was going away in the distance, and we passed a couple of my properties along the way. I thought to myself, *I'll never spend another night here*, and it turns out I never did.

As the ambulance drove off, I thought about all the dreams that had been diminished due to my drinking. I knew that this was the harvest of sowing many bad seeds through many years. It occurred to me at that point that I had lost everything. I had lost my wife and children, my farm that I had worked so hard to get, and my businesses. At that point I wasn't sure if I would lose my life or not. After all those years of my living up there in the big house, looking down on the world both physically and theoretically, my drunken arrogance had convinced me that I was King of the Mountain. Now I realized that I was just a Fool on a Hill.

2 Growing Up in Indiana

I WAS BORN TO PLAY BASKETBALL. In Indiana, it's a birthright. This is, after all, the Hoosier State, home of the finest high school basketball in the world, top to bottom. It's where every high school team, regardless how big or small the school, through 1997 played in a single-class statewide basketball tournament. They call it "Hoosier Hysteria," and even though the statewide tournament now features multiple classes, it's still vintage March Madness.

I had the breeding to play basketball. My dad had been a star high-school athlete, and that included playing hoops. I had the height (I was over six feet by the time I got to ninth grade), and I had a good grasp of pretty much all the requisite skills—I could handle a ball fairly well, starting with being able to dribble with both hands. I was a good shooter, could play smart defense and set picks with the best of them, and could pass the ball. I knew how to block out, get position under the boards and grab more than my share of rebounds. What I didn't have was the desire to keep playing after I hit my teens. Basketball just wasn't in the grand plan for Michael Steimel. Being a teenage alcoholic can derail most anything.

I was born in 1969 and raised in southern Indiana, the middle of three boys. As tired and cliché as this sounds, I was the typical boy from a small Midwestern town. Nothing about me really stood out—except my height and, as I got a few years older, my ability to put away the beers. That was something I could handle with the best of them. There were no zebras (basketball game officials) around to call fouls on me or a coach to stick me on the bench.

Before I hit drinking age—which, for me, was about thirteen—I grew up playing Little League baseball, earning Boy Scout merit badges, fishing, and camping, among other things. I came from a large family, which was to be expected considering that my dad's side of the family was Catholic. That's the thing about Catholics—they know how to kneel and knock out a rosary, especially during Lent; play Bingo, crank out the babies; and put away the alcohol, seven days a week in many cases. My kind of people.

My mother always told me I had a big heart and would make a great priest someday. We attended church every Sunday without fail, but with a guilt-ridden conscience (like most Catholics). We occasionally left behind the burden of our sins in the confessional so that we could take communion every Sunday and scoff at those who attended Mass only twice a year—at Christmas and again on Easter, figuring those were two holy days of obligation they couldn't miss. It was in church where I learned about the love of Jesus and forgiveness for our sins.

So, you might wonder, just how big was my family? In terms of extended family, big enough. There were forty-seven of us grandkids, with me being one of the youngest. That explains why I spent my growing years attending weddings, graduations, anniversary parties, and other family gatherings. I would watch in wonder as the adults drank, danced, and generally lived it up. That appealed to me; it looked like a lot of fun. I decided at a young age that the day would eventually come when I would be able to drink and join in on the fun. Nothing complicated about that; there was always alcohol in our house. Dad kept beer in the fridge, although he generally drank only when friends came over to the house, or when he went out with friends. At times I would think, *Wait until they get a load of me when I'm all grown up, and getting loaded myself—eventually even legally.*

All in the Family

My dad, Sam Steimel, never quite outgrew his high school sports stardom, even after he had served time in Vietnam after high school. Folks around town knew who he was, in a good way, and that bought him plenty of chips that he was able to cash in over the years, so to speak. Dad was a likable guy, and he had some pretty good connections. But that time he spent fighting in a losing war for America did take something out of him—something hard to put a finger on. Sometimes I think my mom and other people would say that there was a part of my dad that never came back from Vietnam. I think all servicemen who served over there returned home the same, scarred in mind, if not also on body. In our case, the man who came back was not the same man our mom married, although in our household she would have been the only person to know the before and after of Sam Steimel.

Because my granddad was a World War II veteran, my brothers and I grew up knowing about the military and had a keen awareness of what it meant to be a veteran beyond just what you see at public events on Memorial Day, the Fourth of July, and Veterans Day. I'm a very patriotic, love-my-country type of person, and active-duty service men and women win my respect and gratitude. In case you hadn't guessed it, you would never have seen me kneeling on the sideline during the playing of the national anthem before a ballgame. No way, no how. That's disrespectful toward our flag, our country, and the men and women who have served time defending our country.

After Dad came back from Vietnam, he got a job at the power company, which was located about an hour away from our house, and that's where he worked for thirty-three years before retiring. He worked electrical substations and got to come home only on weekends because it was just too far to go back and forth every day. My parents decided to move closer to where he worked. So they loaded up the truck and moved to Sullivan, Indiana, where I still live. It wasn't a year later when Dad got transferred and was now working an hour and a half away, so then we would only get to see him on weekends. He would stay in a hotel for which the company paid. It was hard seeing him only on the weekends. Every boy needs a male authority figure in their life. No exceptions. I know that firsthand.

An Affinity for Alcohol

Dad liked to drink. He liked to go out with his buddies and have a good time, socking away the drinks. A lot of times people would come over to the house. There was always beer in the fridge, and he would also smoke cigarettes like a freight train. Those smokes ended up killing him: lung cancer. Often when he went out with his buddies, they would drink while playing cards, usually poker or some other form of gambling. Sometimes they would come over and play these games at our house, as well as at other places. Dad was all in whenever and wherever there was a card game to be had. Whatever the circumstance, there would often be a lot of guys at our house all drinking beer. And I was allowed to watch, as were my brothers. Even at five years old, if

I wanted to take a swig of beer, I would just drink it straight out of Dad's glass, can, or bottle. He didn't care.

My dad's parents had a total of twelve kids, and from those dandy dozen came those forty-seven grandkids. I was like number forty-two on that long list, so I grew up with a lot of older cousins, and some of them were old enough to be my parents, so finding someone in the family old enough to buy me and my friends a six-pack or whatever was never much of a problem. There were few, if any, in the way of deterrents to keep me from drinking all I wanted, and at times I wanted a lot—of course, I'm talking about when I was older, in my teens. I was not doing that sort of thing when I was five. There's got to be a line drawn somewhere, right?

Anyway, growing up, that's pretty much all there was for me—a dad who let me drink his beer and who loved sports, plenty of relatives around, and wedding dance after wedding dance, graduation after graduation, reception after reception, party after party. Growing up, that's all it was for me. At my first communion, after it was over, everyone came over to the house to party, and everyone just drank beer. The amazing thing isn't that I became an alcoholic; it's that there weren't more alcoholics in the extended family. And that's just counting the nearly four dozen cousins, let alone all those aunts and uncles.

Dad and Mom, and Their Three Boys

Dad was always pretty good to me. He wasn't one of those fathers who got drunk all the time and beat his kids; nothing like that. No way. While he wasn't setting a great example for my brothers and me as future grownups and family men, he did take an interest in what we were doing. He was especially interested in seeing us do well in athletics, particularly basketball. Not every kid I knew growing up could say that about his dad.

He spent time with us, just as a good dad should do with all his children. What made it easier for him and us three boys was that Dad was a sports fanatic. He had been the consummate jock in high school, and his interest in sports and sporting activities never seemed to wane. It was a language he knew, and he knew what he was talking about when he would talk to us about sports or how to handle the basketball or get it into the hole. We were playing organized basketball at the YMCA by the time we were in elementary school, and as soon as we could walk he also had us playing baseball.

My parents grew up about five or six miles apart from each other, went to the same high school, and got married a couple years out of high school. My dad grew up on a farm, the eleventh out of twelve kids in his family. They were a Catholic family, a very poor one—they didn't have indoor plumbing until my dad was about sixteen years old.

Dad was twenty-one when they got married, my mom twenty. Voted most athletic in his high school graduating class, Dad had a basketball scholarship to some college in Georgia, not sure where, even though he was only about five-ten and a half. But he was also a good baseball player and a runner. As for my mom, she came from a middle-class family and had one sibling, a brother who was ten years older. Hers was a good family, good people.

After they married, Dad worked in a factory for a while, then got drafted. I tell the story of how I actually saved my dad's life before I was even a year old. I was born in September 1969, and he went to Vietnam three months later, in December 1969. Sometime during the following year (1970), I got deathly sick and spent a month in a hospital while the doctors tried to figure out what was wrong with me and what they needed to do about it. Eventually, they didn't think I was going to make it, which is why my dad was brought home from Vietnam. Dad was a reconnaissance sergeant in the jungle, right in the middle of the "stuff" (action), as they say. Obviously, I survived, but when Dad went back to Vietnam, he found out that he was the only member of his unit or team still alive. The rest of them had just been wiped out on a mission, so his coming home to see me saved his life. That's pretty amazing, although he never talked much about it, and I understand why.

As I was growing up and playing ball, Dad and I were always out in the backyard playing catch. When we moved into a new house, he put up a basketball goal for my older brother Steve, younger brother Tony, and me, and we wore that thing out several times over, over the years. There was some decent height in our family as Dad's uncles were about six-foot-three or six-foot-four—my dad not quite as tall as them, but every bit the athlete.

I had other outdoorsy interests as well, and I did a lot of fishing and hunting with my grandfather. Dad went hunting some, but he was big on other sports, especially basketball and baseball, and he watched sports on TV until the day he died, at age sixty-five. When he was younger, he also traveled around playing a lot of slow-pitch softball, and he would also play in adult men's basketball games until he was into his thirties.

Dad never outgrew his having been a sports superstar in high school, and if there was a party somewhere in the neighborhood, he was sure to be there as the center of attention. Plus he was a good-looking guy, and that, too, played into his grabbing a lot of attention when he was out in public. He never really grew up, didn't have to. All the attention bestowed on him was sufficient validation to him that he was living his life the way he wanted to, and he wasn't going to change—or grow up. Now that I think about it and still picture Dad, he reminds me of the character Dennis Quaid played in the 1979 coming-of-age movie *Breaking Away*, which happened to be set in nearby Bloomington, Indiana, home of Indiana University. *Breaking Away* is about four guys just a year or two out of high school, referred to disparagingly as "townies" by the snobbish university students they sometimes come into contact—and conflict—with. Quaid's character Mike is essentially the alpha-male leader of the group, a star quarterback in high school, who is gradually finding out he's a relative nobody outside the community in which he grew up, now that his days of playing under the Friday night lights are forever in his past. In a way, that was my dad, except his main sport was basketball.

As a dad, my father did have his limits with us, where he would get mad at times, but he wanted to be more our friend than a father. There wasn't a lot of discipline, not nearly as much as there should have been. When we boys got to middle school and then high school, he would let us drink. His being gone because of his work as well as his nights out with his buddies played into that. I'm not laying all the blame for my drinking problem on him, but having a dad who would have put down the law and not allowed us to drink from his beers (for starters) probably would have made a big difference in our lives, especially mine.

Experts have long known that alcoholism is a destructive disease. While the effects of alcohol abuse are experienced by the person afflicted, and struggling, with the disease, they can also be felt by those who are close to the sufferer, such as their children. In fact, according to American Addiction Centers, a child is particularly "susceptible to parental influence and neglect. As a result, growing up with an alcoholic parent can have serious consequences in both the short-term and the long-term. Having an alcoholic father can have a significant impact on a child, putting them at risk for a multitude of problems during childhood and into adulthood."[1]

---

[1] Editorial staff, "What Are the Effects of an Alcoholic Father on Children?," americanaddictioncenters.org, March 31, 2021, https://americanaddiction-centers.org/alcoholism-treatment/alcoholic-father, viewed April 25, 2021.

Citing statistics compiled and published in Psych Central, American Addiction Centers also points out that close to 30 million children have an alcoholic parent, putting them at higher risk of becoming alcoholics themselves. Note, however, that having such a parent who's addicted to alcohol is no guarantee that their children in turn will develop the disease. There is hope. "Alcoholism in the family home can have a significant impact on the most basic operations of the family," American Addiction Centers continues. "Families dealing with alcoholism have been shown to experience problems such as lack of communication, little to no structure in the home, increased conflict, subpar parenting, isolation from the community, and financial issues."[2]

The problems potentially facing children living in households where alcohol use and abuse are significant issues can also include trust issues that can eventually lead to an inability to form meaningful and intimate relationships later on in life. That can also be accompanied by abandonment issues. Perhaps this helps explain why, as a teen and young man, I often struggled with what I now know to be anxiety and depression issues, for which I was at a loss while I was going through those things. I didn't know what was going on. Having such hindsight can't help me go back in time thirty to forty years to know what was going on then, but it's certainly something I've been aware of in recent years. Counseling has helped me to negotiate my way through parenthood and at least make an attempt to keep those issues that befell me as a youth and young man from being passed along to my two daughters, now in their early twenties. I pray about that often now, knowing that I can't do, heal, or fix anything without God's intervention. But as I write this, I am thankful to say that I have been sober going on two decades now.

---

[2] "What Are the Effects of an Alcoholic Father on Children?"

Then There Was Mom

My mom's name was Judy, and her story was mainly putting up with Dad, who until the day he died was a boy in a man's body and clothes. When he came back from Vietnam in his twenties, he brought with him some stuff such as jewelry he had taken off dead enemy soldiers. Mom eventually got rid of all that stuff. She had grown up with good, caring parents and wanted to take care of things, like keeping the house clean and as straightened out as she could, without hoarding a bunch of junk. That could be a real chore for my dad and three rambunctious boys. Make that four, counting Dad.

I think my mom thought she was marrying a farm boy when she married my dad, but he didn't want anything to do with farming, although I had aunts and uncles who did that. My mother also liked to do some outdoors things, like going camping, but my father didn't really want to do that either. For one thing, forty years ago you couldn't take a TV with you to watch baseball or basketball games while on camping trips—not like you can today. What a lot of folks call "camping" nowadays has nothing to do with real camping. Heck, at many of today's campsites, you get to "rough it" by staying in a cabin, complete with kitchenette, full bathroom, and even a shower in some cases. Times have certainly changed. You might as well go stay in a Hampton Inn down the road.

Mom had it hard. Dad was running around some, and they had some trouble between them, marriage issues, although they never divorced while we were growing up. They would divorce twice after all of us boys had grown up and left home, but eventually remarried a second time while my dad was terminally ill.

I'll say this for Mom, beyond just what she was able to do in handling things with her husband—she was very dedicated to us boys. Yes, she went out with my dad, dancing and doing other social things, but her main focus was on Steve, Tony, and me, and we were a handful. Three big, athletic guys with a penchant for life in the fast lane—small-town style—and with loads of macho coursing through our veins. Yet, she was sort of reserved, not someone who would yell her way through the trials and tribulations of everyday family life, but she had our attention. For one thing, and this was all because of Mom, all three of us boys could read even before we got to kindergarten. She taught us how. That was a pretty rare thing, at least back in the seventies; in fact, I was the only one in my whole kindergarten class who could read. Also note that we didn't have a preschool back then, either; there was nothing to prep us for the "rigors" of what was to come in kindergarten.

Our teacher would write something on the chalkboard in front of the room, and I would read it aloud as soon as she was finished writing it. The first time I did that surprised the heck out of her. "You can read that?" she said, turning around to look at me, and I said, "Well, yeah." She hurried down the hall to see my mother, who was a teacher's aide at the same school. Almost out of breath, she said to my mom, "Did you know your son could read?" Mom proudly said, "Yes, I taught them that." She just spent a lot of time with us, mostly individually. It paid off, obviously, at least in some ways. Not everything "took" as well with us, or I should say, with me. We boys are our mom's whole life. She has never remarried since losing Dad almost ten years ago. She dated one guy for a little bit last year, but she's pretty content, although she does miss my dad.

My Grandparents

I was real close to both my grandparents on my mom's side, especially my grandfather. I spent a lot of time with them. Grandpa was always taking us fishing or camping. Anytime there was something going on like a sporting event he wanted to see, and if they were in town, they attended. They never missed anything us boys did.

When we got a little older, Grandpa started taking us hunting. As the years went by and he got a little older, the roles were reversed, and I would return the favor by taking him hunting with me, and he really enjoyed it. As did I. We spent a lot of time together. He was nice and easygoing, as well as very talented when it came to mechanical knowledge. He could rebuild a motor or a gun. Plus, he was a good fisherman; it's no wonder that he had been a Boy Scout leader for thirty-something years. He loved doing things with kids, and he liked sports. He would go to our ballgames.

Grandpa also had a garage with lots of stuff in there to tinker with. It wasn't a really big garage, but it was well-equipped for working on assorted things. He taught me a lot of woodworking skills and how to build stuff, whether it be a birdhouse, a doghouse, or a cabinet. We built picnic tables, too. He taught me a valuable set of skills that made me into a type of handyman, and I developed that do-it-yourself (DIY) mentality from an early age.

Another set of skills that Grandpa had acquired over the years came from his working for a propane company. He was some sort of technician and became quite proficient at converting things that ran on some other kind of fuel to propane. It was a gift. He performed a lot of conversions—cars, tractors, you name it. The sad part of all that is that the propane company he worked for was completely shut down when he was in his late fifties, so he lost his retirement when the company went under. But if he was bitter about it, he never showed it, at least not to me. After that shutdown, he went to work in a sporting goods store, which is where he worked until he was in his late sixties.

Once he retired from that store, he and my grandmother spent a lot of time in Florida because my grandmother had a sister and her sister's husband living in Florida, and there was room for them to stay there. For several years they would annually go to

Florida. They talked for some time about moving there, but they decided they wanted to stay closer to us three boys, so they stayed put in Indiana.

By this time I was twelve years old, and Grandpa and Grandma had moved to a town right down the road; it couldn't have been more than ten minutes away from us. So I got to see them a lot, and we spent a lot of time together. I enjoyed it as much as they did. The previous house they had lived in when I was really young was a smaller, two-bedroom house. That's where they lived for about forty years—just a front porch and those two bedrooms, nothing fancy. Their backyard was small, but it seems like they had everything back there, including a cherry tree, a flower garden, and an actual garden for growing several vegetables they had planted. They also had a grape arbor with more than enough grapes on it to use for making grape juice and even grape wine. It seems like they had unlimited grapes; you couldn't pick them all, there were so many.

I spent a lot of time over at their house until we moved to Sullivan, and that was when I was eight. They were in the town of Bicknell, which is where my mom grew up and where she lives today. It's about thirty miles from Sullivan.

In the summertime my brothers and I would go stay with my grandparents for a couple of weeks. They had a camper and would take us camping with them. It was always a blast. We'd go to state parks, usually not more than an hour or two away. We learned a lot about nature on those trips, and that has stayed with me over the years; I'm still very much a nature person who loves the woods. I love all the outdoors, for that matter. I love the water, especially ponds. Although I'm not a fanatic about fishing, I do like to fish some. I also love the fields and creeks. My grandparents instilled all that in me. Now I know why my mom loved the outdoors so much and always looked forward to the next camping trip. I don't hunt anymore, but I used to hunt quite a bit. I liked to hunt deer, squirrels, rabbits, and birds such as quail. Even though I have quit hunting, I still like to go into the woods. I feel a lot of peace and serenity there, and have never been afraid of the dark, no matter how deep into the woods I go at night.

A Shared Love of Talk and Music

As you might have guessed, Grandpa and I talked a lot with each other. He loved music and was a music buff. When a tune came on the radio or TV, most likely he could name it and who performed it, and with any luck he might even name the year it had come out. He had one of those old reel-to-reels set up as well as an eight-track, and there was plenty of great music to be had sitting there listening alongside Grandpa. One time he figured he had enough reel-to-reel recordings to play music for a year straight without hearing any one song repeated, at least not a version performed by the same particular singer or group. He had recorded that much on tape off the radio.

I followed his love for music as well. I'm a music person. I love listening to music. As soon as I get in the car, I turn on my music. My favorite music is old country. Hank Williams, the Carter Family, and Jimmie Rodgers, all the way to Merle Haggard and Waylon Jennings. I'm not really big into all that stuff they call country today, because it really isn't country. Most of it is just rock or pop music sung with a twang, and oftentimes even the twang isn't there.

I like *good* country music. Willie Nelson is another one of my favorites. I had that on CDs back when CDs were popular, before things like Bluetooth and Sirius XM came along. Haggard is by far my favorite. I like George Jones, which is understandable since Merle and he recorded a lot together over the years. Johnny

Cash, Charlie Daniels, and a lot of other old country musicians are high on my list as well. Even some of the *really* old stuff.

I also like classic rock. I can go from Johnny Cash to Aerosmith in a heartbeat. Being a child of the eighties, I also like a lot of the hair bands, such as Poison and White Snake, as well as some of the alternative stuff from the nineties. Being a Christian, I've also gotten into Christian rock—Casting Crowns is probably my favorite group, but I like Sidewalk Prophets as well. Their lead singer David Frey is from a nearby town. They come every year and perform there. He went to the same high school my daughters attended, but he's a lot older.

My dad liked old country music, too. He was raised on a farm, and every Saturday night his family would watch the Opry. They would also listen to or watch *The Porter Wagoner Show* when Dad was growing up. My dad didn't have any equipment with which to tape and replay music, but he listened to the radio. We took vacations every summer, going one place or another, and I can remember growing up and all summer that radio was blaring out "Coca Cola Cowboy" by Mel Tillis or songs from Merle Haggard or Johnny Cash. Anywhere we went with Dad, we had country on the radio. This was before we kids got to middle school, by which time he would let us play what we wanted to listen to.

My mom was a child of the fifties and sixties. She had a lot of 45s she gave us when we were young. They featured Elvis and Buddy Holly, stuff like that, so I have a love for that kind of music, too. There were also Marty Robbins, Conway Twitty, on and on.

Grandpa was also into cameras and photography, and he was a terrific photographer. Just writing all these things about Grandpa, as well as my grandmother, brings rich memories rushing back into my head, and I sometimes find myself smiling through the tears. It's a great feeling, and I have no regrets for any of those moments spent with them. Not one iota. Grandpa had his own photography shop for a while, so he was always taking pictures. Most of the pictures I got from him were most likely taken by him.

As I end writing this chapter of this part of my life, I am obligated to tell you that my grandparents—my mom's dad and mom—weren't drinkers. That part of their influence never took hold of me, I am ashamed to say. Grandpa didn't drink at all, which is a testament to his character, because his father was an alcoholic. Grandma drank once in a great while—maybe a glass of wine or a beer once every several months or maybe even once a year.

Grandpa was an intelligent man, and I credit him a lot for who I am today. He was a Christian, and a firm believer in me and all that I did. He constantly told me how good I was at everything I did, and how proud he was of me. He told me of a dream he had of me getting and staying sober, because he knew of all the trouble it caused. It never came to pass during his lifetime, and I actually was drunk the night he passed.

One of the last conversations we had before he passed was about life. I asked him what he had discovered about the secret of life. He said "it" isn't a secret. "All you have to do is get right with the Lord," he said, "and everything else will fall into place." I wish I would have taken heed to his advice then, and not kept going like I was. I was able to give a eulogy at his funeral, and though he's been gone many years, I still visit his and my grandmother's gravesites whenever I'm in the area.

My grandfather was aware of my drinking. I think by the time I went to my first rehab, my grandparents were well aware of how bad it had become. But, no, we never really talked about it. When I was in rehab, they came to visit me every weekend. When I started drinking again after that first rehab, my grandmother said she was disappointed in me, but I think that was the only thing either one of them ever said to me about it.

I don't know if it would have made any difference had either of them ever sat me down to lecture me on it. Probably not.

3

High School Daze and Drunken Nights

I DISCOVERED ALCOHOL AND its debilitating effects (both in the moment and for the long haul) when I was thirteen. One sick way of looking at it is that at least I waited until I had crossed over into teenhood before getting smashed for the first time. By today's standard, I was a late bloomer. More and more, you hear about kids ten, eleven, or twelve years old—even younger than that—hitting the bottle hard. I take no pleasure in knowing that I held out a couple years later than they did. I would love to be able to help every one of them.

My first real drunk came in the summer of 1984, when I was fourteen, at Sullivan County Park and Lake. I made a deal with my dad that if my brother Steve and I painted the house we could go camping at the lake. After Steve and I painted the whole outside of our house, Dad drove us out to the lake and dropped us off close to Campground F, where a lot of older kids would go and party. A friend, Todd, came with us. We got some older kids to go buy a case of Michelob beer, in cans, for us, and that's how we got drunk, easily drunk. Sometime in the middle of the night, Todd and I went for a swim in the lake, and when we got back, Todd got sick in the tent. When Dad came back later in the morning to pick us up, he helped us take the tent down and clean up our area. When he opened the lid to the garbage can to toss in some trash, he saw all the Michelob cans in there but didn't say anything. So ended the first of many, many drunks for me.

I believe I was an alcoholic from Day One. When I was intoxicated, all my worries left me. With a few beers in my system, I wasn't shy, I wasn't stressed, and my anxiety and depression issues disappeared. The other side of the coin is that whatever problems of mine were sitting it out during a night of drinking, they would come pounding back at me the next day, and they had only gotten worse.

By age fifteen, I was drinking any chance I got. I showed up for my first day of high school drunk, and did my best to stay that way the next four years. Every weekend I was searching for alcohol, and I would get grouchy, or testy, when it wasn't available. I had to be intoxicated to feel like I fit in, especially before I went to a school dance or any other event. Because of alcohol, I gave up basketball and started running with a new group of friends. My sports friends didn't want anything to do with me, which was fine because I really didn't care about them anymore, either. I was in a bad way.

During my senior year of high school, I missed fifty-six days of school—Ferris Bueller had nothing on me, and I was under the influence most of that time. I knew that I had a problem, but the booze was the only thing I felt I could rely on. My parents and I were often in conflict with one another, and I couldn't wait to get out, even though I had nowhere to go. Yeah, I didn't mention that earlier when introducing you to my family, but Sam and Judy had their issues, and my hanging around the house sober for any of that just wasn't in the cards.

By the spring of my senior year of high school, it had become evident that my alcoholism was getting worse. I went to my parents for help, and ended up in outpatient rehab. I went to professional counseling for a few weeks, but I soon returned to drinking (but not to school). I chose not to attend school for any of my final exams; I didn't care if I graduated or not. Somehow, though, (I believe out of sympathy of just not wanting to deal with me anymore), they passed me, and I got my diploma. Twenty years later, a former teacher told me that I still had the detention record at my high school. At least I was remembered for something.

By the summer after my graduation, which was in 1988, alcoholism had taken over my life. I was drunk every night, and started missing work and experimenting with illegal drugs. In August of that year, after a long drinking binge, I again asked my parents for help. I can still see my dad sitting with my mother in the swing out in the backyard when I again went to them and told them I needed help. Dad's reply was, "We will do whatever it takes to help you."

So I checked myself in to inpatient rehab, and spent thirty days trying to get sober. After rehab, I became active in a twelve-step program and managed to stay sober for a couple of months. I was actively attending church again, and doing the things I needed to do. It wasn't long, however, before I started hanging out with the same old friends, going to the same old places, and eventually ended up back on the sauce. That was the easy part—falling back into the same old trap, one from which I just couldn't stay away. There's a saying in the twelve-step programs: "You have to change your people, places, and things." Obviously I failed to heed this lesson.

Once I had eked out graduating from high school, my only goal in life was to get a decent job, buy a little bit of land, and settle down with a good lady and, eventually, a bunch of kids. My dad had worked many years for the power company, and I would've been quite content to follow in his footsteps. I quickly found out, however, that jobs in our area were few and far between. I must have applied a thousand times to various places, with no hope for employment.

That's a pretty quick summary of my high school years and what I was facing immediately after graduation. Before I go any further, though, I'm going to walk back the narrative and reflect more on my high school years, elaborating to give more insight into what happens in the life of a teenage alcoholic. Some of you might remember back to a fifties movie—or at least maybe you heard of it—*I Was A Teenage Werewolf.* It starred a very young Michael Landon, who would later star in a couple of very successful, long-running TV shows: *Bonanza* and *Little House On The Prairie*. Well, I was no teen werewolf, but I Was a Teenage Drunk. If anyone ever wanted to make a movie about that, the screenplay is already done. I know because I lived it.

Miss May

As much as I disliked school by the time I got to high school, I hadn't always been that way. I actually liked school up until the third grade. That came to a halt when I got a teacher who had been my brother Steve's teacher the year before. Her name was Miss May. I never knew or cared to know her first name, which is typical for schoolkids, at least back in that era. Miss May was an old maid who had never married or had any children, which is probably why she couldn't understand why I wasn't like Steve, who was very well-behaved and a great student as well as a good athlete—a well-rounded guy, no question, a fact which for years irked me to no end.

Steve could do no wrong; I could do nothing right. Whatever fondness for school I had had before I got into Miss May's class, she burned it out of my system. Scorched-earth mentality. I began to hate school, and to this day I still despise classroom learning. My parents made several attempts to switch me to another teacher and class, but the school administration in its infinite wisdom wouldn't budge. They were more about making kids tough it out instead of making even a modest effort to find a solution for me. They were totally uninterested in doing what was best for my long-term growth and enhancing my educational opportunities. I ended up becoming a failing student throughout the rest of my school years, which became the core source of conflict and stress in my young life. Yes, I am to blame for much of that, but I had plenty of "help" along the way, no thanks to my schools.

By the time I became a teenager, I was searching for anything that would allow me to find my own identity. Something positive to call my own. I was in constant conflict with my parents over my grades, and because I also hated school, I didn't feel like I belonged anywhere. There was nowhere for me to go—no safe place for me to find peace and fulfillment. My being so stressed and depressed in middle school brought on various physical ailments. At one point, all my eyelashes fell out. What the heck was that about? I was taken to a pediatrician, who ran multiple tests and did some lab work. After all known possibilities had been checked, I was diagnosed with stress—plain and simple stress. That shouldn't be the predicament of a thirteen-year-old boy, but I was having suicidal thoughts even at that young age. Back then, anxiety and depression weren't ever mentioned; putting a kid on that type of medication was unheard of. Many times, though, especially through adolescence, I felt this way.

Steve

Part of my problem, too, was how I was always being compared to Steve, as I followed right behind him in school, our just being about a year apart in age. That wore on me over time. Despite our being so close in age, we were worlds apart when it came to ambition and achievement. Steve had it all over me in that regard. While that sometimes bugged the snot out of me, I never yearned much to close that gap, even a little, even though I tried some. In fact, I was constantly struggling to keep up with him. He was a straight-A student and a good athlete. I was always being reminded of that, and even though I was always one of the biggest guys in my class, I felt small. Mr. Underachiever—I got straight As in that class of Inferiority Complex I. My teachers, coaches, and other adults were always comparing me to him. This would turn out to be an unending debacle I had to deal with most of my life. I was already shy and never seemed to have my own identity, other than being "the older of Steve's two younger brothers." The other was Tony, who was two years younger than I am.

Steve now lives in the Dallas area. While he doesn't remember many of the details from his high school days, he does recall being the most driven of the three brothers in our family, striving to achieve great things and hoping to go places in his life. No argument from me in that regard. He went on to become valedictorian of his high school class and earned an appointment to the United States Air Force Academy. He dropped out of there after about a year and three months to go to Indiana University, home of the Hoosiers.

"Yeah, I was really driven back in those days," said Steve, who agreed to contribute his thoughts and memories for this book. "I think Mike bore the brunt of it (the expectations from others, such as teachers) a lot of the time, and maybe I just had more direction at that point in my life, more guidance. By the time I was in the seventh grade, I had decided I wanted to go to a service academy. So I spent the next five years of my life dotting every *i* and crossing every *t* to make sure I got in. I knew what I wanted to do and how I had to do it. I drank less than Mike did because I had stuff I had to do, and it was important to me. I don't know if Mike had the same kind of direction in his life, like what he wanted to do or where he was going.

"I was always a dreamer and a schemer, always wanting to accomplish something, in some way, shape, or form. It was a little easier for me to buckle down and focus when I needed to because I had something to focus or move toward. I don't know that Mike had that. Our parents always gave me pretty much free rein, because I'd make straight As. Plus, I earned Eagle Scout. I guess you could say I was really good about playing the game. I would get away with stuff, and Mike not so good. He was always a little bit of a black sheep, and I was getting As in school. My parents catered to me a lot, while they struggled with Mike and he with them to a certain extent. It wasn't like they were ever unkind to him, it was more just pushing him, like 'C'mon Mike.' I'm not saying Mike was a problem child, but I'm sure he was getting to the point in his life where he was like, 'What's the use of fighting this fight?'"

Although Steve and I were on opposite ends of the achievement and accomplishment spectrum, we were good friends, at least for the most part of our young lives growing up with one another. It did get testy at times once we were both in high school. If I had any bitterness about him, it was that others had this lofty opinion of him, almost like they idolized him, although he wasn't one to tout himself or pat himself on the back for all his accomplishments and honors. Some of those times in my early teens when I was already drinking, Steve was there with me.

Steve again:

"Our parents never really let any of us boys stay at other people's houses or do anything like that (staying out all night), but what they would let us do was go camping. They would take us out to the lake or wherever to a campsite, drop us off, and then we'd get somebody to get us beer after our parents had left. When I got my driver's license when I was sixteen and he was fifteen, we'd drink every chance we got, usually just out in the woods, somewhere nearby."

Our fun times weren't solely centered on drinking.

"I remember one time," Steve said, "when we were probably in junior high. We were down at Buck Creek and were determined to build a cabin. So we started chopping down this big tree. It took us about a week to cut through it, probably because we had a dull hatchet. The tree looked like it should come down but it wouldn't. So Mike climbed to the top of it and started shaking it. Well, the tree came down while he was still in it. I don't know how high it was, but it was pretty tall. Mike rode the tree down and it hit the ground, where it bounced (recoiled) and threw him up in the air, and he then landed on the ground. 'Oh, my God, he's dead!' But he was fine."

It's ironic how Steve mentioned that story because it's true. I liked to climb things and wasn't afraid of heights, and that played into my career building and putting up cell towers in hundreds of places around the country, many of them several hundred feet high.

Drink Up

The only thing I really excelled in was basketball while in school, and that carried a lot of weight in a state whose iconic legends include the likes of John Wooden (the great UCLA coach, a native of Indiana), Bob Knight, Larry Bird, and Norman Dale—the latter the fictitious coach portrayed by Gene Hackman in the classic movie *Hoosiers*, which also starred Dennis Hopper and Barbara Hershey. I sometimes wonder if it was coincidence that all three of those actors had last names starting with the letter 'H' so as to be in sync with the movie's title.

Most of my friends were the boys I played basketball with. The fact that I was tall—I grew to be six-foot four, although Steve insists I'm more like six-five—and the fact that I had been playing since I was old enough to walk, were advantageous for me and helped me outperform others. Still, I felt insecure, being the younger brother to Steve, who was so accomplished in his own right. When I was drunk, everything seemed to be fine. It seems like that's all I ever wanted.

Any chance I could get alcohol, I would get it. There was some in the house, but not a whole lot. My parents didn't know I was swiping it for myself, and I didn't get caught until I was fourteen or fifteen. They thought it was the first time for me when they finally caught me, but it was more like my twentieth. By age fifteen it had a hold of me, and I didn't want to do anything else. I didn't want to go out or do much of anything without first having some alcohol to get me going. The friends I had by then were drinking, too, but it wasn't affecting them like it did me. We all might have looked the same in doing it, but we weren't. I noticed that when we went out and couldn't find anyone to buy some alcohol for us—obviously we were well below the legal drinking age, which was twenty-one—I would get real antsy and irritable, much more so than any of the other guys I was with. They were chill about it. While my friends got a kick out of drinking, to them it was just something to do; to me it was something that I needed. I tried smoking weed one time when I was fourteen or fifteen, but it didn't do a lot for me. I liked the alcohol too much, and when I did smoke, I would end up falling asleep.

There was one time between my freshman and sophomore years when a friend and I went to a party where there were a lot of older kids. It was a pool party at the city pool and they had what they called "jungle juice" there—Kool-Aid mixed with Everclear.

They allowed my friend and me to join them, even though we were only about fifteen. So we mingled and drank.

Eventually, the others decided to take their party elsewhere, to a big campground by the lake, a place that offered boating, swimming, and other activities and amenities. It was a spot where a lot of people partied. Here's the thing: my friend and I had told our parents that we were staying at the other's house, but here we were, ending up out at that lake. He had his license and I didn't, and the other people there were between eighteen and about twenty-five. Once again, my being big for my age was the ticket in.

There was a patrolman at the lake checking things out, making sure there was nothing bad going on, and he also happened to be one of my school teachers. This was how he picked up some extra money during summer break from school. He also was a good friend of my dad's, and they bowled together. Plus, he was my track coach, back when I was also doing track and field. Somehow my dad figured something was up and went looking for me. Dad ran into this guy, who, of course, knew exactly where I was, but he sent my dad off in another direction, away from the party, and then came and got me. He took me to meet my dad; I'm sure he figured that taking me to my dad would be bad enough a fate for me yet less than going to jail, so he kind of covered for me, too.

I ended up grounded for a while, not sure how long. Maybe it was just a few days or a week? At times like this I would usually end up on the receiving end of an hour-long lecture from my mom and dad. Typically, when I was drinking, I also had a chew of Copenhagen in my mouth. My dad would stand there with a beer in one hand and a cigarette in the other and say to me, "You know, you shouldn't drink and you shouldn't chew." I never called him out on that. Never said a word.

Sometimes I would be hungover the next day, but I could handle it pretty well. All the lecturing in the world wasn't going to do any good at that time. My mom wouldn't get too upset and would try the motherly approach on me. It never worked, either.

Hoop Dreams? Not Exactly

If you love basketball and there's any state you want to grow up in to cultivate that love, it's Indiana. But you already knew that, right? I had it made. I started playing basketball at about age five at the YMCA and was pretty good from the start. By the time I got to junior high, I was one of the better players in my hometown for my age group. I still occasionally see my junior high basketball coach. He'll mention how he still has the scorebooks from those days and will refer to them and tell me, "You know, you really lit it up and led us in scoring about every game. You never should have given it up." He's right about the scoring part. I did lead the team in scoring most of the time.

Up until the time I made drinking my No. 1 and only sport of choice, the friends I had were really into sports. When I got to be a high school freshman—we had both a freshman team and junior varsity, in addition to varsity, of course—I knew if you were really good, you'd move right up to the junior varsity team, and that's what they asked me to do. But I turned it down because I was insecure; this tied into my other problems that led me into and sustained my drinking. I didn't want to play with the older kids (mostly sophomores and maybe a couple juniors composed the jayvee team) until I knew I could handle it. Beginning my freshman year, I was pretty sure I couldn't. No jayvee for me.

So I played with the freshman team. At the same time, I got a failing grade in a physical science course, so I had to sit out. No more basketball for me; I wasn't eligible to play anymore. That just reinforced now much I hated school. My drinking was part of that, but so was having a teacher like Miss May back in third grade. I remember I really got into it with her when I was about nine years old, and she seemed like a hundred then, and she made my life miserable. I finally told her, "Someday you'll be gone," or something like that, and she said back to me, "Well, I might just outlive you." Long story short, she lived like into her late nineties. She almost did outlive me. In fact, I think she would have if that bullet to my head had killed me.

My last shot at continuing to play basketball came during the summer following my freshman year. I went with my best friend to Bobby Knight's basketball camp at Indiana University, although I didn't get to meet the legendary, hot-tempered coach affectionately known as "the General." I think he appeared only once during the whole week I was at the camp—they just use a coach's name for that sort of thing, to help promote it. Toward the end of the summer, though, I just lost all remaining interest in basketball and didn't want to play anymore. Although Coach Knight got blamed for a lot of stuff over the years and ran off his fair share of players at IU, he had nothing to do with my giving up on basketball. It wasn't his fault.

I waited until the fall of my sophomore year to tell my dad I wasn't playing basketball anymore. It totally broke his heart, considering how much he loved it and how good a player he had been in high school. It also broke the heart of my best friend's dad, who had been our coach in seventh and eighth grade. He also talked to me about it, trying to get me to stick with it, but it didn't change things for me. Here I was now a sophomore, and going to practices and playing games with juniors and seniors really bothered me. Anxiety had a big part to do with it. Fear of failure maybe? There was a part of me that didn't want to make a commitment to a team sport that would require me to stop drinking, or at least curtail it significantly.

We also had a new head coach that year, and that, combined with everything else, just scared me, although I'm pretty sure no one noticed that about me just by looking at me. It's not like I was having anxiety attacks, at least not at that young an age. Also, Steve was being pretty mean to me at times and would bully me. He was just a bully at times. Most of the time growing up we were like best friends, but he was stronger than I was and could beat me up any time he wanted. By the time I had gotten to sixth grade, I had passed him in height, but he was still intimidating because he was older and did so well in school. I didn't do so well and was constantly being told I was stupid—and that was accompanied by lots of sarcasm and some disparagement.

I was pretty reserved and quiet, but at times I was also a class clown and cut-up, and I got into some trouble at times at school. Other times, trouble was waiting for me, and it occasionally included Steve. He talked down to people, including me, of course. He was somewhat arrogant, which contributed more than anything to my insecurity. I believe he thought of himself as funny, but he wasn't. Plus, it was just tough following him through school with all the successes he had. In some small way it was something like being the coach who immediately succeeded the legendary Wooden at UCLA, a guy whose teams had won ten national titles in a twelve-year stretch and more than 80 percent of their games overall. A tough act to follow—I know what it feels like.

A Need for Counseling

I didn't know it at the time, or at least I didn't accept the idea, but I needed professional counseling beyond any twelve-step program. I had no mental counselor or therapist to work with me in identifying my problems—starting with putting a name to them—and then learning how to cope with them, to include being properly medicated.

It wasn't until years later, while I was married, that I finally started getting some counseling. That just wasn't the sort of thing that a kid in his teens or his parents would reach out for, at least not in the eighties—almost like it was taboo; counselors and therapists were for other types of people, not us. Sometime after I married Joanna, I was referred to counseling because it was thought I might have clinical depression. My wife told me to go to this place where I was told I had this and this and this. That was a huge deal, a shock to me, hearing all that stuff about me. Even just twenty years ago, this sort of thing wasn't as well-known or the treatments as advanced as they are now.

I was put on some sort of medication, and by this time I was about thirty years old, now going to counseling and taking medication. The thing is, though, you can't be taking an antidepressant and then be drinking a depressant such as alcohol, because that defeats the whole purpose. Even with the drinking, the depressants I was being prescribed at age thirty still helped, and I got a lot a lot better. It got even better once I stopped drinking, which was close to twenty years ago now. If only I had known then (while in high school) what I—and medical experts—now know.

I go back to when I was thirteen and having anxiety issues and who knows what else, leading to my eyelashes falling out. Mom sent me to a doctor, who thought it was just anxiety and stress. When we got back into the car, I asked my mother what stress was, and she said, "It's when you worry a lot." I told her that I didn't worry a lot, and she asked me what I worried about when I did worry, and I said, "School, for one." I probably had depression, too, even back then. I'm talking 1982 or 1983, back when no one talked about a kid having depression. I've never talked about any of this with my brothers, but I've learned alcoholism is hereditary. Both of my brothers drink, but it's not my place to go into that in any detail here. That's their business, and I'm just going to leave it at that.

All the time I was going through high school, I don't think I ever had a fake ID like some guys did, but I was able to get served for the first time when I was seventeen, still four years under the legal drinking age. I remember walking into a tavern down the road from where we lived. I was with a friend and we figured we would try it, so we walked in and then I walked out carrying a cold six-pack—yes, paid for. I was not into shoplifting, although I'm not sure how you shoplift a whole six-pack at once. I was not about to try.

I got served at the tavern for a long time. Then, by the time I was eighteen or nineteen, there was a liquor store down the road that would serve me. Plus, the closer I got to twenty-one, the more friends I had who were twenty-one, although there still were days I couldn't get ahold of anything to drink quick enough to suit me. Those were the days, or nights when I would get really irritable, and it felt like the day had been wasted. I hated going home sober. I had a hard time sleeping on those "wasted days and wasted nights," although I was sleeping pretty well anyway, until it started getting worse a few years later.

By the time I was sixteen, I was running around with a different set of guys who were not as into sports—at least not basketball—as the guys I had hung with before. The friends I played basketball with were more sports-minded, more straight arrow. The guys I ran with throughout the rest of high school liked to do the same thing I did, which was to drink, and a lot of them also liked to smoke weed. A lot of them played sports, too, just not basketball. Some, or most, played football. So, in different years of high school, I was hanging out with different guys. By the time I was a junior and senior, if they weren't drinkers, they weren't hanging out with me.

I've had people I know come up to me in recent years and say they know I drank but had no idea I drank as much as I did. Even those who were close to me say this, which shows that as much as I ran around and drank, I did a pretty good concealing it from most people. Put it this way: I wasn't hanging out on street corners under the streetlights drinking while advertising it to the world. My buddies and I would get our hands on what we were going to drink, then find someplace we could go drink in relative peace and privacy. No one tried to intervene with me or anything like that, except my parents on occasion.

Rampant Detention

I dated off and on in high school and had a girlfriend for part of my senior year, but never had a steady girlfriend much of the time in high school. I met Joanna at the end of the spring my sophomore year. She was a year behind me in school, and we dated part of the time.

Being absent from school for those fifty-six days I mentioned earlier wasn't because I was sick or anything like that. I just didn't go. My parents both worked and were out of the house before it was time for me to leave to go to school, so they didn't see me not going to school. I was either going hunting or fishing, but most often just drinking. Something to take the edge off, you know?

Even when I was actually at school, I wasn't physically in classes a good chunk of the time. Chalk that up to how our lunch periods were scheduled. Things were different back then; for lunch you could go wherever you wanted, as we had open campus. They had what they called A lunch and B lunch. If you had A lunch, you had three classes and then went to lunch, which lasted thirty minutes. Then there was a twenty-minute gap. B group would go to four classes and then lunch following that twenty-minute gaps. Add it up, and that's a total of eighty minutes for the two lunch periods and the gap in between—call it an hour and a half. That was right up my alley.

When I dropped my fourth class, I was to be assigned to a study hall in its place. The guidance counselor asked me if I wanted A lunch or B lunch. That was so we could determine which study hall I would go to—before lunch or after lunch. He said to just show up for one or the other. I took it a step further: I didn't show up for either one. I had A lunch (thirty minutes), then the twenty-minute break, then I had B lunch (another thirty minutes). With that near hour and a half, I was off to the races. My girlfriend had the A lunch period, and I would hang out with her, then go hang out with my buddies for the twenty-minute break plus the B lunch period. Or it might have been vice versa. It doesn't matter. I was a free bird either way.

I did this for several months, but finally got caught when my grandmother called the school one day and left a message for me (no cell phones in those days). Her call came in during the fourth period. Whoever was bringing the message to me was supposed to take it to me at my fourth-hour class, either the class I had dropped or the study hall, but I wasn't in either one of them. Busted! I was told I was going to have to make up all that time, and it added up to something like 165 hours of detention—and that's in addition to the fifty-six days I ditched school. As it turned out, I didn't make up a single minute of it. On top of that, I got out of school at 1:30 every day for something called work release, and I didn't even have a job. About ten of us guys would go drinking or fishing (or both), or whatever else seemed suitable on a given day. A full day of school for me was supposed to be five hour-long classes (more like fifty minutes each, actually) plus two hours of study hall, but I really had only three class hours for the whole day. Bottoms up!

One of the teachers who was there when I was in school is now the superintendent of the school district. He's a great guy and jokes with me every time he sees me: "Thirty years later and you still got all this detention that you owe me," he says, grinning. But I got passed, and I graduated. Dad was friends with the principal, and he bowled with my econ teacher. My senior year, the last semester, I didn't take a single final exam, and they still graduated me. I guess they just didn't want me back. My scorecard from senior year shows fifty-six days of absenteeism, 165 hours of detention, and no finals taken. Plus the accumulated work-release hours. I also had some days in there where I got suspended from school, although I don't remember what it was for. I probably cussed out one of the teachers.

Still, my senior year was the best year of my school life. Steve had gone off to the Air Force Academy in Colorado Springs, and I was finally my own man. My parents and I got along better that year than we ever had. My younger brother, Tony, was a sophomore my senior year. He ran around with me some and missed some school, but nothing like I did. He would go on to be voted most athletic in his class. I should have been voted most absent in my class. Maybe I was, but just wasn't present to hear about it. I just kind of fell through the cracks, and my parents didn't know where I was or what I was doing.

My Best Test Turned Out a Bust

You know how I said I struggled in school, was a terrible student, and just didn't care? Well, school wasn't actually that hard for me, but I had another experience when I was in ninth grade that alienated me from school more than even Miss May had. I was in an algebra class that I didn't care about, and I wouldn't do my homework. My dad figured out what was up with me and algebra, and he had a long talk with me about it. A halftime pep talk of sorts.

The algebra teacher was a defensive coach in football, and I always thought he was kind of an ass. In discussing algebra with me, Dad talked about it for a long time, essentially telling me "You can do this," while also encouraging and trying to motivate me in other ways. My own Tony Robbins house call. I said, "Yeah. I'm going to do this, and I'm going to try." We had a test coming up in a few weeks, and I actually studied for it. It wasn't that hard for me, so I didn't have to study that much, but I did what Dad had asked me to do and got well-prepared for the test. I took the test, and I aced it, the only one in the class who did.

The teacher graded all of them and gave everybody their test back, and I saw that I had aced it. He then picked them all back up, and ripped them in half in front of the whole class and said, "We're not going to count this one."

I wanted to say, "Screw you," but didn't, even as crazy as I was. I held back. I went home and told my dad about it, and he bowled with this guy, too, and wanted to say something to him about it, but I begged him not to. I didn't want any future repercussions from it. And that was it—I was done. I think I might've made Ds and Fs the rest of the year, but this was the kind of stuff that really turned me off about school.

Still, I look back now and know I was blessed to have a lot of really good teachers—teachers with whom I'm still friends today. I've been out of school for thirty-three years, and some of these teachers are some of the best people I have ever met in my life. But there were also a lot of teachers who weren't. Most of the teachers I'm friends with are in their seventies or eighties; when I see them today, they give me a big hug and get one from me in return. Some of them have been supportive of my doing this book and speaking at places. A few have even gone out of their way to come hear me speak and that's the kind of stuff you can't put a price on.

By end of my senior year in high school, I got tired of all the drinking and wanted to quit. That's when I went and talked to my parents about it, and they sent me to that outpatient clinic, and I got some counseling. I went to counseling once a week for about a month. My mom took me, but she didn't go in with me to see the counselor. I stayed sober for a few weeks, but I always wanted to drink like normal people, even though I realized I *couldn't* just drink like normal people. That's the reality of alcoholism. By the end of that summer, I was out of control; I knew it had me. So this time I checked myself into inpatient rehab, trying to get sober. A counselor tried to get me to go to AA meetings, but I wouldn't go and wouldn't even hear of going. I wanted to do it my way. That's what I thought, anyway.

I spent thirty days in the rehab unit, which was located about a half hour from home. My parents would come to visit, and a lot of my friends would come by, too. Nobody sneaked me any drinks. Rehab workers didn't pat anybody down coming to visit a patient, but what they would do is take the patient's vitals twice a day to keep tabs on them. If you were drinking anything sneaked to you, they would find out. They took your blood pressure and temperature. It wasn't tortuous for me. When I came out of there after those thirty days, I felt really good, like I had a new lease on life. I turned nineteen about two weeks after I got out of rehab and I was going to AA. I was also going back to church and things were pretty good.

Here's one more story, an uplifting one, I want to share pertinent to my years in school. Back when I was in high school, in the eighties, I was a terrible student and didn't want anything to do with it, as you know. My junior year a new teacher came to our school. His name was Mr. Clements, and he was a football coach as well as a first-year teacher. He and I butted heads mainly because of my bad attitude. We were definitely adversaries, both junior and senior years.

Fast forward twenty-nine years to 2017. I went back that year to my high school to share my testimony and speak to the entire student body and faculty. As I began my talk, one of the first things I said was that back in the day I had an attitude problem and didn't do well or get along, especially with teachers like Mr. Clements, who, it so happens, was still on staff twenty-nine years later.

I gave my talk and testimony and shared with everyone like I normally do when I speak. After it was over, and all of the students had filed out of the gymnasium, a few of the teachers hanging around came up on stage to chat with me. One of them was Mr. Clements. He shook my hand and told me he was proud of me. I see Mr. Clements occasionally to this day, and he always says hi to me and is always friendly. It's amazing how things can turn around, back in the same place I started but definitely on a different platform than the one I was on twenty-nine years earlier.

4
Man at Work

GETTING THROUGH HIGH SCHOOL was a breeze thanks to all the missed days, skipped classes, blown-off finals, drinking, and a faculty and administration that figured it best not to put up a stop sign for me. So far, so good? Not in my case. The flip side of being out of high school was that it was now time for me to find a real job and get to work—not a great prospect for a drunk flunky-should-have-been.

I never did do my time for the one thousand-plus hours of school detention I accumulated, but now I was serving a different kind of detention—no job. At least not a full-time one. Being eighteen years old, depressed, drunk, and jobless is no way to go through life, son. I also was living in a depressed area of the Midwest; the only work I could find was farm-related. Nothing against farms or farmers, but this is no way for an eighteen-year-old guy to begin a career and start making a living for himself—and, presumably, making a living sufficient to support others if I were to get married and start having children. Growing up on a family farm is one thing, but a part-time worker just out of high school and without farming experience had better keep his resumé updated (even if there wasn't much to be added to it).

I spent many hours on the tractor and in the hayfields during the farming stint. Other than that, I generally just stayed drunk most of the time. Although I tried college a couple times, I couldn't stay sober long enough to attend class. Instead, drinking and driving became my normal. I also, again, gave up on church and my Christian life. It is said the first symptom of alcoholism is denial, but that was never the case with me. I never denied the fact that I had a problem. I just accepted it and tried my best to manage.

Many times I came home intoxicated. I remember a certain late night when I missed a curve and drove head-on into a large drainage ditch, my head busting the windshield on the driver's side. Nothing out of the ordinary about that, for me. But the strange thing was that even though I was by myself, there was also a head print that broke the windshield on the passenger side. Soon a deputy sheriff was on the scene, and it took me the longest time to convince him that I was alone. There was no one there, and based on what was done to the windshield, it's inconceivable that a passenger would have been unable to sneak away that quickly. Part of me believes that Jesus was riding with me that night, although even he must've had a heck of a headache if that had been him sitting up front with me. Once again, the police let me go, without any charges. I was valedictorian in the school of enablement. Everyone just kept letting me go—teachers and sheriff's deputies alike. A charmed life? Hardly.

By the age of twenty I was willing to go anywhere to find work. Unemployment, or even underemployment, is no place to be. Not for anyone who cares. Whatever job or career awaited me, I knew for my own good it had to be in a new environment with new people and circumstances that would allow me to get sober. I also realized, though, that addiction follows you wherever you go, and that is a real bugger, believe you me. A new environment in a different town will only provide a temporary pause in the addiction process, at best. The one constant was that it was me in my shoes, and dealing with my addiction was all on me. Keep that in mind if you are an addict, whether you are a drinker or doper, your only ultimate solution is yourself. If anyone is to blame, it's *always* you. My constant abuse of alcohol, accompanied by depression, anxiety, and hopelessness, made for a miserable life. It was only the beginning of a personal battle that would last for many years.

Climbing the Towers

Jobwise, I finally got a break In the summer of 1990, around the time I turned twenty-one. God had answered a prayer, although I don't recall the last time I had actually prayed for real. That door was opened for me when I met a couple young men from New Mexico who worked for a communications tower company. A contract job had brought them to Indiana, where they were working for a local company doing some work on the company's towers.

One day they happened to walk into the building of the power company for which my dad worked. They said they were looking for some local help and asked around if anybody knew anybody wanting to work, someone who needed a job and could handle what they were doing. There was a guy working at my dad's company who not only knew me, he also knew I was looking for work. That night he called me and told me about these guys, suggesting I go see them the next day. So that's what I did. I went there the next day, introduced myself, and said, "I heard you were looking for some help." They told me they were and that they needed someone who could basically dig ditches for conduit and electrical wires that needed to go underground. They asked me when I could start, and I told them, "Right now." They said, "Here's a shovel," and I think I worked harder that day than I had ever worked in my life. I made a very good first impression. I was a bona fide worker bee.

These guys were joking with me throughout the day, saying, "You must be part Mexican because of the way you dig." I worked there a few days, after which they told me they had five more of these jobs in various locations around Indiana, and asked me if I would go with them for what would be several more weeks of work. I liked the sound of that. So I traveled with them around the state, working hard and enjoying it. Once we were done with all those jobs, they asked me to join them back in New Mexico, which would mean I'd be getting into the tower business. I said I'd think about it, and off they went, back to New Mexico, their work in Indiana finished.

A few weeks later I called them up and said I had decided not to start college—I had registered for classes at Lincoln Trail College, in Robinson, Illinois.

"So are you going to come out here and work with us or not?" they asked me, essentially inviting me to move to Albuquerque.

It's not like I was bolted to the ground in Indiana. Joanna, my high school sweetheart, had gotten married two years earlier and moved up somewhere on the East Coast. I thought it over for a few weeks, and eventually concluded I had nothing to lose. It would be a chance to travel, make some money, and maybe slow down or even quit the booze. Looking back, you'd think I would have immediately jumped at the offer and the opportunity to work full time, even on a short-term contract basis, without hesitation, but as eager as I was for a good full-time job, I had some trepidation about moving away from southern Indiana. I still had plenty of homeboy left in me, as well as the comfort of being able to drink with people I had known for years.

I accepted the offer and my parents put me on a Greyhound bus, said good luck, and I was on my way. This was about a week before my twenty-first birthday, and all I had was a suitcase and a little money in my pocket my dad had loaned me. At the bus stop, Dad's handshake was firm, and Mother's tears flowed as she gave me what would be her last hug for a while. With a head full of dreams, I boarded the Greyhound, and I can still remember crossing the Wabash River and thinking, *My life will never be the same.*

Once I got out West, I actually climbed my first tower on my twenty-first birthday, September 20, 1990. Even though I obviously didn't know anybody, things went pretty well. The company paid for my hotels when we traveled; the first couple of months saw us going to a lot of places in New Mexico and Arizona, and then it was up into Colorado. Eventually, we worked our way farther north into the Seattle area for a while.

I learned quickly that putting up towers was something different and very dangerous. Back then, some thirty years ago, we didn't have the kind of safety equipment that is available today. You're free climbing the whole time, with nothing to hook on to until you get to where you're going on the tower. Once there, you're hanging several hundred feet in the air, although at twenty-one years old, you don't think about it much. You don't dwell on the dangerous aspect of it; you don't think about anything. At least I didn't. That's the mindset you want to have when you are doing that all the time. The more you think about it, the worse it can be for you. Don't look down, right? Afraid of heights? Find another job. You stay focused on the job at hand—what it is that you are supposed to be doing at any given moment. Do that and you don't have time to be scared. Just don't do anything stupid or play daredevil. If you do, gravity awaits, and it's relentless.

One thing about this industry that revolves around erecting and working on towers is that the only time you read much about them is when it's bad news, such as a tower collapsing or a worker falling and being seriously injured or killed. At the heights we typically work on, several hundred feet in the air, gravity can really do a number on you. I don't need to be an expert at physics to know the ride down can have an abrupt ending, and *ending* is the right word. I've Googled it and found that if you fall from a height of about three hundred feet or more, you are going close to a eighty miles an hour by the time you make contact with terra firma, to put it mildly. Imagine standing in the middle of a road and getting hit by a Mack truck going eighty. Same thing, pretty much.

One mishap in 2020 comes to mind; it has been referred to as the "Alabama Miracle." According to wirelessestimator.com, two men working on a 349-foot tower in Seale, Alabama, were injured when the tower toppled, apparently because of failed rigging, dropping the mount on a guy wire and collapsing the tower. The two tower techs were tied off at 225 feet on the AT&T tower, which was being decommissioned when it came down. The men had no choice but to ride the tower down because they were attached to it. At least it wasn't a free fall, although the fallen tower soon turned into a mass of a twisted torrent of steel into which the men landed as they came down. One of them walked away with some bruises on his body, while the other was hospitalized with leg injuries that easily could have been much worse.[3]

---

[3] Wireless Estimator, "Sadly, 2020's Top Stories Were Fatalities and Structural Failures," December 30, 2020, wirelessestimator.com/articles/2020/sadly-2020s-top-stories-were-fatalities-and-structural-failures/, viewed January 4, 2021.

After my New Mexico coworkers and I finished up in Seattle, I headed home at Thanksgiving for a few days, then it was back to New Mexico, where we headed out cross-country to Virginia Beach. Then, for me, it was back home to Indiana at Christmastime for the holidays, and then back to Virginia Beach. It involved lots of travel, getting a chance to see the country, and I was liking it. Still drinking, of course, but I was liking what I was doing. There was hope for me.

I was making six dollars an hour. That's not so great money—remember, too, this was about thirty years ago, and six dollars then is probably equal to double that now—which still isn't that great, but when you are working eighty hours a week and all your hotel and meals are paid for, that's not so bad. The only downside was that I spent every penny I made on drinking and partying. There were times, on my days off, that I would sit by myself and drink till I passed out. For a kid in his early twenties, though, I had a lot of money saved up, proof positive that I had not thrown away all my money on booze. Every minute that I wasn't working, I was drinking. We all drank and went out partying. The other guys liked smoking weed; me, not so much. That wasn't my thing; drinking was. Still, I smoked occasionally with them.

At one point we were working for a contract company out of Chicago, and by then I was ready for a change. I wasn't real happy with where I was. I had been doing this long enough to see that we were a smaller company, and soon I got a chance to go to work for a bigger company based out of Chicago. I didn't hesitate to take the offer, and this was in January 1991. It was closer to home for me, less than five hours away, so I jumped at it.

My career was taking off, and I wasn't going to hesitate when a promotion or a better opportunity came available. I was employed with the Chicago company for a couple years, and my career really took off. I worked nationwide and even spent some time in Mexico. Eventually, I was promoted to supervisor. I was still drinking every chance I got, and would stay drunk until I had to report to work again. Any money made was generally spent on my lifestyle. Other than the booze, I spent a lot on gambling and women. Many times I would wake up not knowing where I was or whom I was with. *God* was not a word I wanted to hear. It got to the point that I didn't even want to discuss Christianity or have anything to do with it.

It was a better company to work for—better money, better benefits—than I had been working for in New Mexico, not that New Mexico was bad. It wasn't. They opened the door for me, and for that I am forever grateful. The Chicago company paid all my expenses plus they gave me a company truck, which I used to travel all over the country, everywhere from Virginia Beach to Seattle to Texas, working different jobs in different areas.

None of the jobs lasted very long, maybe a few weeks or even only one day at a site. We were doing cellular at a time when the cellular industry was just taking off. I didn't even know anybody who had a cell phone yet, that's how cutting edge this all was. We were working on cellular towers pretty much all the time. Back then there were only a few towers in any one area, compared to now, when there are thousands of towers in every area of the country. We had to travel to where the work was, our well-paid assignments to install antennas, cables, and electronics. It wasn't nearly as complicated then—it's a lot more technical now and takes a lot more technical knowledge.

A Stranger Back Home

When I came back home to Indiana to visit my family and friends, nobody had a clue what I did, what type of work I did, and they didn't know anything about it. I could have told them I worked for NASA and it would have made just as much sense for them—

none. But that was as much about it being such a new industry as it was their living in what was basically Podunk, Indiana, without a great sense of what was going on in the big world around them. I would tell them I was working on towers basically.

It turns out my friends and people really didn't want anything to do with me when I came back home. I detected a little bit of jealousy because I had made it on my own out of town, out in the world. I might just as well have been Columbus. A lot of times in a small town, people never make it out. They live their whole lives there. They go to school; they graduate from school (most of them, anyway); and then they get married and have kids, and the cycle starts all over again for the next generation. They never see anything or go anywhere, whereas I'd been out to all these cool places and done all these things all over the United States. We no longer had anything in common.

The change was on me as well. I had a different mentality then than I do now. I was also a different person than when I left because I had been in the business world, had traveled around, and had seen different things. I wasn't the same small-town kid that they all knew. Even the guys or gals who went from high school straight into the service (army, navy, air force, etc.) didn't see anywhere near the breadth of the world—at least in America—that I had seen. If you go into military service, you go one place for basic training and then get stationed somewhere else on a permanent assignment. Then you eventually get out and, in most cases, go back to where you grew up, and sort of pick up where you left off. Basically, my old friends didn't want anything to do with me.

Then there were the casinos that beckoned when we were on the road fulfilling contracts. These casinos were legal only in selected areas of the country, such as Las Vegas, Atlantic City, or Biloxi, Mississippi, or on or near Native American reservations. We ended up working a lot in Atlantic City. Anytime I was there, I was gambling. I liked to gamble and throw money away on blackjack and slots, especially. I'd win a little bit here and there, but never enough to cover my losses. It was the same thing with women. Sometimes there were hookers. They weren't hard to spot, and they certainly had no difficulty spotting an easy mark like me from a mile away. A lot of times when a guy is traveling with money in his pocket in these different towns, women aren't hard to pick up. The ones I met were nasty, and I'm sure they were doing with me what they had done with a thousand other guys before I got there. Barflies. Luckily, I never came down with a sexually transmitted disease.

I worked all of 1991, part of that time in Mexico. I was down there for a month or so, and it was a whole new experience. I didn't speak a lick of Spanish. Then there was the matter of trying to find my way around the country. After a while down there, I started noticing a worsening problem with my knees, which had been troubling me from time to time since I was in junior high. That was rooted in my having grown too fast when I was younger. Only now, the discomfort—and eventually pain—had gotten to a stage where it was starting to affect me at work, hindering my ability to climb up and down those towers, and my bosses knew it. Finally in September that year, it was decided I needed arthroscopic surgery on my knees—one operation in October and the other in December 1991—and I wasn't able to go back to work until February 1992. Problem is, my knees still hadn't healed very well and I was in a lot of pain. I climbed for another month before it got to be too much. Finally, in March 1992, I decided I wasn't up to snuff for what was needed to climb those towers day after day, so I returned to Indiana. Once I was back home, I just kind of bounced around and stayed drunk most of the time. There weren't a lot of jobs around and not as many factories as there are now, at least not in our area.

The surgeons who had performed my knee operations had advised me against climbing towers anymore, which pretty much made me useless for that sort of work—there wasn't much to do for a guy with two bad knees who was told he couldn't climb anymore. That was the most essential part of the only job I knew how to do. It's like a basketball player with bad knees accompanied by surgery being told he can't play basketball anymore. If you can't run up and down the court and jump dozens of times a game, how can you be of any use to your team?

I was devastated. Back in Indiana, I was depressed, unemployed, and, of course, inebriated half the time. I'd grab a cold one out of the fridge, knock it down, then get another, and then another. Life goes on. I was able to get an insurance settlement from the Chicago company, but it didn't take long for me to drink it away. So there I was, back where I started, with no options on the table. It would be like I had never left, right? Maybe New Mexico, Chicago, and all that good pay had just been a dream. I returned home a stranger, however, as though I had been away on Mars the whole time. I no longer fit in back home. I had become too "worldly," I guess is the best way to describe it. People at home didn't relate to me, and the feeling was mutual. That started me on a downhill spiral that lasted nearly two years and escalated my alcoholism to a new level.

I was living at my parents' house, but spending most of my time at the local watering holes. The more I drank, the more I became depressed, and vice versa. I had filled out applications at numerous companies, with no luck. As all this was going on, I was missing the tower business more and more, and I craved a return to the road.

Many times while out drinking, I would be pulled over by the local police and somehow managed to be let go each time. I was spending time in less-than-reputable places with less-than-reputable people. Early one morning, after a long night of coon hunting and beer drinking, my brother, Steve, and I were involved in a severe accident. This was December 1992. We were outside of Sullivan on the way out to our parents' house, about six miles out of town. We were on a two-lane highway, and I was driving. We'd been out drinking all night although it wasn't daylight yet.

I was driving a full-sized Chevy pickup and somehow crossed the center line, where we were hit broadside by a truck traveling at a high rate of speed. I don't remember a lot of the details, only that somehow we ended up sideways in the middle of a highway and the other truck T-boned us, smacking right into the driver's side door. The impact pushed me over into Steve's lap, and it knocked me out for a bit. I'm not sure how long, but it felt like only a few minutes. When I woke up, I asked Steve what had happened. He said we'd been in a wreck and the back window of the truck was broken out. We climbed out through the back window because we couldn't open either of our doors. I jumped off the back bed of the truck, not knowing I had a broken pelvis. It didn't really hurt me because I was in shock, but I took just a couple of steps and then had to lie down. Steve wasn't really hurt, although one of the two guys in the other truck had a broken leg.

As the four of us lay in the middle of a dark highway—these other two guys had apparently crawled out of their busted-up truck as well—a tanker truck came into view and was heading straight for us. My brother was able to shine his hunting light just enough for the driver to lock up his brakes at the last moment. As the semi-truck slid sideways and missed us by a few feet, the hunting light crumbled in my brother's hand and never worked again. Another car came through, and didn't see us in the road. The driver frantically swerved through the accident, missing each of us by a few inches. I remember the feel of the car's tire as it grazed my ear.

The first officer on the scene was a young guy with whom Steve and I had grown up. He was panicking. He had worked the riots in Los Angeles (Rodney King, etc.) while he was a deputy sheriff there, but his wife had wanted to move back to Indiana. He saw me lying there bleeding out of my mouth, and he kind of freaked out. That was understandable. He said it's so different when it's one of your friends you come across in a wreck. One of the things he had learned working in Los Angeles was that when somebody is bleeding out of their mouth, it usually means they're not in very good shape; it's serious. The ambulance came to haul me away, but Steve refused to get into the ambulance. He wasn't hurt at all. The guy in the other truck with the injured leg ended up sharing the ambulance with me.

They took us to the small-town hospital near where we lived. My brother told them to call his wife because he was supposed to meet her that morning to go somewhere. She was staying with our parents because they didn't live in the same town in which we lived. So our parents and my sister-in-law came to the hospital, and the doctor said it was serious. I had internal bleeding, and the staff there didn't think there was a whole lot they could do for me. They went ahead and x-rayed me and discovered that I had a broken hip. They didn't know what other internal injuries I had, so they transferred me to another hospital thirty miles away in Terre Haute, the next city over, where I could get a more thorough examination. I spent a week at that hospital, and, thankfully, everything started healing up okay. I then went through physical therapy and spent several weeks walking around on crutches and with my neck in a neck brace. I guess my internal injuries weren't so bad after all, because I didn't need any surgeries or anything like that. And I stayed sober for a little while. Maybe it was three weeks that I went without drinking, then I was right back at it.

I hung around our little town for another year—staying drunk most of the time. I still wanted to get back in the telecom business, but didn't have any options or places to start. Toward the end of the year, I had given up on returning to the telecom industry, and decided I would attend college and pursue a different career. I was to start college in January, studying electronics at Ivy Tech Community College, and was preparing my life for a new direction. In December 1993, though, I got a call from a contracting company out of Atlanta, asking me if I would be interested in taking a management position in Argentina. It would be a white collar job, paying nearly six figures, and not only would put my career back on track, but also take it to the next level. After much thought and time spent discussing the opportunity with my parents, I decided to pass on college and move on with my career.

I had been referred to this company in Atlanta thanks to some connections I had in Indianapolis. By then the company in Atlanta was building cellular systems throughout Argentina and pulling together everybody they could with any experience to go down there. My name was in their database, which is how they got ahold of me. It had been almost two years since I had been in the business, between the time my knees had given out in Chicago and now. I was twenty-four years old, and it turned out I would be making about five hundred dollars a day.

I accepted the job offer and headed for Argentina. South America, here I come. When I arrived, all I had was an address. I knew no one and spoke no Spanish, yet I somehow managed to find my way around and eventually was placed in a remote area of the country by my employer. Even a five-star hotel in a third-world country is not much to get excited about, but I soon became adjusted to the culture and comfortable with my position. For the most part, all I had to do was drive around and check the status of towers being built. It was a simple task and allowed me to stay drunk during my six months there. I eventually found the "lower" part of town, where the booze flowed, the whores were abundant, and the drugs were readily available. I spent a lot of time in those places—even though I always knew it wasn't right. I was hooked. A few times I would try to take a break from that lifestyle, but would manage to stay sober for less than a day.

I paid my expenses out of my own pocket, which wasn't a problem. My pay was $300 a day and expense reimbursement $200 a day, so I was making $500 and staying in a nice hotel that cost a lot less than it would have cost in the United States. Argentina was nice, but poor. I was making in a day what most people I had met there were making in a month. Plus, the government was corrupt. Soldiers would stop people and only let them go once they gave the soldiers some money. It was a mixed bag that the job lasted only six months, which is when they let me go.

The contract expired after about six months, and I had nowhere else to go except to head back home to Indiana once again. I got there at the beginning of summer, and I had money in my pocket, thanks to Argentina. I had no problem staying drunk the next three months and sleeping with any woman who would have me. Occasionally, the drinking would lead to a bar fight, and someone always got hurt. Even though I was quite capable of holding my own, I never felt like I actually won. By the end of that summer of 1994, I had managed to stir up enough trouble around Indiana that it was suggested by a sheriff's deputy that I move out of state—quickly.

Once again discouraged, I called up a friend I'd worked with in South America, and he offered me a position managing a telecom division in Atlanta. Without hesitation, I packed up and moved south to Georgia. This would be the first company I had managed, and I soon learned the great amount of responsibility involved. It was a big company looking to branch out and start its own telecom business, and they were hiring professionals to help build things. So I went down there, along with a friend. I was assigned to manage one of their tower crews, contracting for a company in Kansas City. I hit it off pretty well with those folks in KC even though I was planted in my office back in Atlanta. They liked me, but I soon found out that the KC company didn't like how my company conducted its business, particularly in terms of their methods and procedures. After a couple months of this, they suggested that I start my own tower company and then subcontract with them. I didn't have a clue about how to run a business, so in February I went back to Indiana and talked to my dad about starting my own telecom company.

Going into Business for Myself

I had always dreamed of owning my own company, but I lacked the knowledge and financial savvy at that point in my life to be doing this. By now it was early 1995, and that was when my dad and I started discussing plans for starting my own tower communication business. I was going to push ahead regardless of my inexperience in some areas of running a business. We met with various small business counselors and explored some of our options. I decided to offer my two brothers a chance to partner up with Dad and myself. So, in March of 1995, the four of us started our company. My dad already had a career with the power company, so he remained a silent partner with my venture. My brothers, Steve and Tony, were twenty-six and twenty-two, respectively, and I was twenty-five at the time. I had about five years' tower experience while my brothers had zilch, but none of us had any business experience. We had very little capital, and started with the bare minimum of equipment.

Neither Steve nor Tony came on board with me at the same

time. First, I had been out with Steve when I clued him in about my new Dad-backed venture, and he said he would like to have a piece of that action, working alongside me. My other brother, Tony, was in Germany going to college at the University of Hamburg (I was never sure how in the world he ended up there). Steve and I gave Tony a call, told him about the new venture, and he told us he would like to get in on it, too. Although we were not really that close to one another, the thought of our teaming up seemed to make sense, especially when I told them that there was money to be made in this business—that much I could vouch for.

I had secured some possible job contracts when I left Atlanta, so we had work from Day One. The company took off and did really well. We were making money, and when we weren't working, we were partying. By the end of 1995, we realized we had something good. The next year we started hiring employees and buying new trucks and equipment. We bought seven new one-ton trucks that year and hired several employees. By the end of 1996, we had become a million-dollar-a-year company. My dream of owning my own company had come true (albeit with two brothers, and all of us equal partners—rookie mistake on my part), and that business was my pride and joy. I spent most of my time, day and night, at my office, either doing paperwork or working in my shop.

I really appreciated Dad's support and enthusiasm for what I was doing, even if I really didn't know what I was doing. Oh, sure, I knew all about putting together towers and putting them up, but I was no businessman. I had never managed people, balanced the books, or done much in the way of delegating things out to others. I had always been a hands-on guy, and a pretty darn good one at that, especially when my knees were in proper working order.

It was learn as we go, but that didn't intimidate me; it just motivated me to learn what I could and to pay attention to what was going on. We incorporated a year later. I knew how to do the work somewhat, but my brothers didn't have any experience. Steve had already been to college and had worked with the same power company that my dad was with. And now he had left there to come work with me. I was the only one with experience and it was tough starting out. We had all the work we could handle, and we had contracts being handed to us. We would sort out things over time, and I saw myself as a quick learner when it came to this field of work.

We were getting all these contracts through word of mouth. People knew we were available and we didn't have to do any advertising. I knew people all over the country from my earlier jobs, and they remembered me. People on the East Coast, plus everywhere from Florida to Iowa, and New Mexico to Texas, and many points in between all of those places were contacting us for our services.

We ended up scattered about quite a bit because of that. Most of our time was spent installing equipment on towers that had already been put together and put up, although we did build a few towers ourselves. In most cases the companies that contracted us to work for them would buy the equipment themselves and have it ready for us to install. That simplified things. We'd get to the site, they'd bring the equipment out to us, and we'd put it up on the tower(s). Then it was back on the road to someplace else. We grossed more than a million dollars in our first year of operation and netted a decent amount off of that.

As good as the money was, it wasn't enough to keep my two brothers and me from coming into conflict with one another. Spats between siblings are nothing new. As most of us know, growing into adulthood seems to exacerbate sibling rivalry, or conflicts, more than it washes them away. The issue with us was when my brothers—neither of whom had one bit of relative experience doing tower work before they came to work with me—wanted to do things differently from what I wanted to do.

Old conflicts between us came out. I felt that a lot of times the work wasn't distributed evenly, and sometimes I would be doing more work than either of them. Dad had put in eleven thousand dollars for us to start the company, and he did that by borrowing against his IRA. Even though we managed to pay him back within two months, our working relationship started going south. There was always some conflict coming out of somewhere, and it was usually between my older brother Steve and me. He was the only one of us who was married, and we had hired his wife to run the office. That was a source of angst as well. Here I was, still only in my mid-twenties, a drunk absentee quitter while in school, now dealing with hundreds of thousands of dollars passing through our hands every couple months and dozens of other tasks and responsibilities, and none of us with enough sense to run a company.

In writing this book, I asked Steve to offer his point of view of what went on with the three of us brothers working together on a venture that none of us was really prepared for. Consider this an attempt on my part to provide, if not full disclosure for this book, at least a fair shake to my brothers in presenting more than one side of the issue. Steve, by the way, was living in Dallas at the time I wrote this book and interviewed him for it:

"I wouldn't say it was a falling out between us," Steve said, looking back. "It's more like we went our separate ways. Tony and I had found the company a good way for us brothers to get back together because, in part, we missed each other—we did. We were all in our early to mid-twenties when we started the tower company, and we were confident in ourselves because Mike had worked in the business for a few years.

"This was also right before the PCS (personal communication system) boom, you know, in like the mid-nineties. Tony was at college in Europe, at the University of Hamburg in Germany;

I was working for a local utility company, the electric company; and Mike was home. We had never gotten to see each other in a while, and we missed each other because we were young. We didn't think we'd ever make huge money, but we'd probably make enough to eat and we'd get to hang out together.

"Things went really well for a while. Two years into this Mike got married, and that kind of changed his paradigm a bit, his priorities. And so Tony and I bought out Mike, and then he started his own side company, a small one doing tower work. Tony and I continued as the remaining partners, just the two of us. I then sold out after about ten years, like in 2004. Tony still continues to run the company today, while I still do contracts. I've worked for Tony off and on over the years, doing tower work and the body still being willing. I haven't climbed for a while, but if Tony has a job here or there that I can help out on, then I'll go and do a project like that, as long as it's within my personal bandwidth.

"The money was coming in pretty easily in those early days, with the business booming, and it just got to be overwhelming."

The development and growth of technology had something to do with that bit Steve says about the business becoming overwhelming at times. In the early years, it was all about voice only—cell phones just being an extension of simply making telephone calls. But then came text and the transmission of data associated with using cell phones for accessing the internet all hours of the day. Steve explains further:

"The more data there is going out, the more information there is being transmitted," he said. "At the same time, towers just can't beam that much data as far, which is why towers have consistently been built closer and closer to one another over the years. That is, the cell sites have gotten closer and closer together, which in turn has called for more buildout and more people to make that happen. With so much demand, you could just name your price. Somebody was throwing any amount of money at it to get stuff up. It was really lucrative at the time.

"I think Mike sometimes got overwhelmed when things got really chaotic. It just seemed a little bit too much for him at times being concerned with the amount of debt you have to carry to finance things such as equipment (such as buying those seven trucks in the same year) and the number of people you have working for you spread all over the country. It's hard keeping track of all that. It's really stressful, you know."

I admit that what Steve says about the stress of managing a company like this did wear on me, but I also didn't get much constructive assistance from my brothers. But I'm not going to get into an argument with Steve for the sake of this book—I appreciate his willingness to contribute some of his thoughts and will leave it at that. I will say this, though: the biggest mistake we made was in setting up our company was treating ourselves as equal partners. Knowing now what we didn't know then, someone should always be majority owner of a company, even if it's just 50.1 percent, and be in charge. The three of us still drank heavily and spent a lot of time in the taverns.

Once in a while we would end up in a violent altercation with others, but somehow were able to come out on top. Also, I was still having run-ins with the law on several occasions, but always managed to stay out of jail. On one occasion, I failed a breathalyzer test and was taken to a hospital for a blood alcohol test to make the DUI official, or they might still have called it a DWI back then. When we got to the hospital, the lab tech felt sorry for me and watered down my blood so I would pass. The officer who had taken me to the hospital had said to me, "All you need to do is pass this test, and I'll take you wherever you want to go. I interrupted your night."

After we waited and waited and waited, the lab tech—her brother was a friend of mine—finally came back with the officer not in the room, and said, "You passed! You passed!" I was surprised. So was the officer when he came in and saw the report the lab tech handed to him. He wasn't very happy at all that I had passed the test. I told him to take me back to the tavern. I found out later through a mutual friend that it had taken the lab tech six tries in adding water to my blood sample before she got it under the legal limit threshold. My percentage of alcohol in my blood was pretty high.

Another time, while on a job in Virginia, I was pulled over late at night after drinking all day. There were several officers there, and they gave me a field sobriety test, which I passed with flying colors. Then they tried the breathalyzer, and I tested .32, which is four times the legal limit. They thought it was broken, so they tried another test on me. Again I tested at four times the limit. Finally, the officer dealing directly with me said he wouldn't arrest me because he "didn't believe I was drunk." He then had my truck towed and called me a cab. Looking back through all the years, I can clearly see all the times God was looking out for me, and there were many such times.

Once my brothers and I started making money, and long after we had paid off our dad's loan, I became more arrogant and drunk even more of the time. I'd go to a tavern and spend five hundred dollars like it was chump change. I left big tips for the employees, and I got to feeling like they needed to bow down to me in a certain way. I just didn't treat them well, period. I was losing touch with my real self, becoming something I wasn't. That's what alcoholism does to you, especially when you are drunk—it puts a different mask on you. You see the world differently—in some cases, alcohol can act like truth serum—and you see people differently, and vice versa. You can become someone other than who you really are, and the real danger is that this might very well be how you spend the rest of your life, with an unwanted alias, unless you take it upon yourself to have an intervention with yourself. That takes the presence, assistance, and patience of other people who know you well, and that list of people was a short one for me.

Soon that short list of mine would include a wife, and eventually things started to go really haywire.

5
Love & Marriage

I MET MY FUTURE WIFE, JOANNA, in the same place where a lot of high school guys and girls connect for the first time—in the bleachers.

I was sixteen and a sophomore in high school when I met her, then fifteen and a freshman, at a track meet. We were on the same high school team, but I hadn't met her, not really. Teammates but strangers. She was some sort of runner, maybe a sprinter, but I'm not sure. I was one of those big oafs who tossed the cannonball—a shot putter. I was sitting in the bleachers killing time and there was another girl there who, as I found out, was a mutual friend. She walked up and started talking to Joanna—I was sitting nearby, and it turns out there was a high school dance scheduled for that night. Joanna was talking to the other girl about it, and then she asked me about it, I guess to see if I was planning on going. And just like that, I now had plans for the evening.

This other girl—the mutual friend—had kind of a reputation for being easy. So that night, after I had had my usual warmup of several beers, I went to the dance looking for this other girl, figuring this would be my chance to score. But I couldn't find her. Instead, I found her friend Joanna—my future wife. I went up to her asking if she knew where her friend was. That turned into a conversation between us, and it just sort of went from there. We ended up dating for a little while, and we dated off and on the rest of the time I was in high school—we were both dating other people as well. We even went to my junior prom together.

Joanna was (and is) a short brunette, about five-foot four—a good foot shorter than I am. She was the middle of three sisters, just like my being the middle of three brothers. At the time Joanna and I started going out, my grandfather was in the hospital and I was staying with my grandmother to look after her while he was gone. Joanna talked about my grandpa being sick, and she was very caring, very nice and sympathetic. That told me she was a very caring person, and that had a lot of appeal to me. Her uncle had died recently, so we talked about him as well. She had really cared for him; we were often comforting each other dealing with the kind of stuff that most teenagers never have to worry or talk about.

We felt a connection, but still didn't date a whole lot that first year. During my junior year, similar deal—we dated a little, but not enough to make anything of it. At the start of my senior year we got back together and decided to date, and we dated pretty seriously. Then a younger girl came along, a freshman, hitting on me and flirting with me, and I took the bait. So I went out with her. That meant cheating on my girlfriend, Joanna—and that was the end of that. It's not hard to find out about something like that in a small town. Joanna and I broke up over that, and that was that. After high school, though, our paths would cross and we would again stay in touch and periodically see each other.

Sometime after high school, another one of Joanna's friends had married young to a guy who was in the navy, stationed in

Connecticut. It was while visiting her friend in Connecticut that Joanna met another guy, also in the navy, and that turned out to be her first husband. After he got out of the navy, they moved to Spokane, Washington.

By then I was traveling around the country and to other countries as part of my job in the telecom business. By happenstance it eventually worked out once that we were both back in Indiana at the same time and managed to get together during some of that time to visit. This was in the summer of 1994, during the time I was working on a contract basis in Argentina. We had been staying in touch, talking on the phone every couple of months, and she would sometimes call my parents first, to find out where I was each time and how to get ahold of me. I also had her work number. Though we had remained only friends—I guess you would call it platonic, maybe even pen pals—we had some very intimate discussions about our lives. We talked about how her life hadn't been what she had expected, and I countered with how fast-paced my traveling lifestyle had become and it wasn't what I had planned, either. We laughed and cried, and cried some more. We then went our separate ways, but still kept in touch and remained close friends.

After a few years of living with her husband back in his hometown of Spokane, Joanna divorced him but decided to stay in Spokane. By then I had moved back to Indiana, where I now had my own company—thanks to my dad's help and with my brothers joining me. She and I had kept in touch, and in October 1996—by which time I was twenty-seven—she asked me to fly out and visit her, and that's what I did. When I got to Spokane, she picked me up at the airport, and we spent a few days together at a luxury hotel I had reserved for us. We had a great time together, and when it was time for me to return to Indiana, the idea of going our separate ways didn't have a lot of appeal for either of us. Still, I managed to pry myself away, departed, and flew back to Indiana, where I went right back to work. We stayed in touch, and in December I asked her if she wanted to fly back home for Christmas. She was thrilled at the thought, not only of seeing me, but also of seeing her family.

A few days before Christmas 1996, I picked her up at the airport in Indy and we started our "Christmas to remember." We spent a lot of time together, little of it practicing good habits. We ran around during the day and drank all night. One late night, after several hours of drinking, I took her to the exact spot where we had experienced our first kiss about ten years earlier. This time, both of us now in our mid-twenties, I asked for her hand in marriage. Without hesitation, she said yes, that she would marry me. The next night we went to my favorite local hangout, and, with this being the holidays, it was packed. I announced our engagement loud enough for everyone to hear and then shouted out that the next round of drinks was on me. It was time to celebrate! That ended up costing me around five hundred dollars along with a fifty-dollar tip. Not a problem, though; not that night. The prospect of getting hitched did nothing to slow down my partying or throwing money around. Quite the contrary, it got me amped up.

One thing at a time, though. In a few days it was time for her to fly back to Spokane. She still had a life and job there, and we both needed to get back down to business. Even more so than the time I had visited her in Spokane a couple months earlier, the hardest part for both of us was saying goodbye. She ended up not staying there very long—the pull between us was too strong. It brings me some pleasure to think back on that time some twenty-plus years ago—happier times, for sure.

We decided it was time for us to be together, for good. In February 1997 I flew back out there, loaded up her belongings, and moved her back to Indiana to live happily ever after with me.

I had rented a small house trailer. We moved in together and started planning our wedding. I was still traveling quite a bit with my job, and occasionally she would go on the road with me. Life was good and so was the partying.

Everyone seemed to have an opinion of what we needed to do for our wedding. We were constantly hounded with suggestions, even though we hadn't asked anyone. Welcome to the world, huh? One Saturday night, we attended a friend's wedding reception. It was then we realized how much effort and money went into such an event. The following evening, we were sitting home again discussing our wedding, when we came to the conclusion that we didn't want all the headaches of a big wedding. We just wanted to get it over with. So, we decided we would make it a simple event the following Saturday, April 19, 1997, only six days away. We invited a handful of people and planned it on the same exact spot—on Merom Bluff overlooking the Wabash River in far western Indiana, right across the river from the eastern edge of Illinois—where Joanna and I had had our first kiss eleven years earlier (April 19, 1986).

We didn't plan it that way, for us to wed on the same calendar date on which we had kissed for the first time, but I guess it was just a quirk of fate. Good omen? Bad omen? Just like at our engagement, and our first date eleven years before, we were drinking when we said, "I do." We found a local justice of the peace to perform our ceremony. After the wedding, I asked him how much I owed him. He told me to pay him whatever I wanted to. So, I handed him two cases of beer and he issued nary a protest.

It was just supposed to be a handful of people for the outdoor wedding—Joanna and her two sisters, and me and my two brothers as well as our parents and our living grandparents (she had a grandma still alive and me a grandpa), but her mom went and invited a whole bunch more people. There were no chairs, no altar, just all of us standing on a spot on the bluff. My two brothers stood with me and her two sisters stood next to her. We were drinking quite a bit before the wedding, my brothers and I having sucked down a few beers at the local tavern. Joanna and I got married late in the afternoon, around four or five p.m. The weather was nice and we guys wore long-sleeve shirts even though it wasn't cold. It was a shirt-and-tie affair, while Joanna wore a dress.

I had done it! I had married my high school sweetheart—the love of my life. For a guy who had spent virtually all his adult life by himself, it was a dream come true. We didn't have time for a honeymoon, though. I had contracts waiting to be fulfilled, and I hit the road just two days after the wedding. I traveled quite a bit for the first few months of our marriage. Once in a while Joanna would go with me. Eventually, we hired her to work in our company office, against my better judgment. My sister-in-law already ran our office, and I didn't want my wife that close to my family. Things went pretty well for a few months, but before too long an increasing amount of conflict between me and my two brothers began to emerge. As always, it was them against me. The presence of conflict wasn't limited to just me and my brothers; eventually, it spread to me and Joanna.

Our marriage was rocky from the start. Chalk that up to one of us being an alcoholic (that was my forte) and the other one working her way there. I drank every day, and Joanna usually had a few herself. I had depression and my mood swings; she had issues of her own but not the kind of chemical depression I had, and I wasn't on medication yet, either. Another thing was that her family was always trying to control us. They lived fairly poor, and we had a nice piece of property we owned along with a big house and new vehicles. My work had been good to me. Her family and sisters were jealous of us, though. Right after we married, I bought her a new Suburban, and a couple years later we traded in that for an Excursion. Her family didn't handle that well, even though it was none of their business. We tried to live privately. We had an unlisted phone number, and we didn't go to too many places where people we knew would see us. Our privacy bugged her family even more. Her mom and sisters hung out with each other all the time, and her mother would go around bashing us to other people. Calling them an annoyance was an understatement.

Even with our problems, though, I really did love Joanna, and I think she loved me, at least in the early going before things really started to deteriorate. We came from different upbringings and held different beliefs in a variety of areas. Money was another issue. I had been making a lot of money in recent years, putting me in a position to buy pretty much anything I wanted when I wanted it, and the urge would hit me time and again. On the other hand, she had come from a family that struggled financially for years, and she was uncomfortable with the manner in which I was dabbling in investments and various other ventures that carried a fair amount of risk, yet with the potential for some nice gains.

By the summer of 1997, however, I was ready to get out of the family business. The ebbing relationships with my brothers and me was taking all of the joy out of work for me and creating the kind of stress with which I didn't want to be burdened. Steve and Tony convinced me to stay, to hang in there, and that worked for a bit, maybe a few more months. Still, it was an excruciating decision for me. I was the one who had conceived the company and gotten it started, and I really loved what I was doing and fulfilling all those contracts and leaving happy customers in my wake. I didn't want to get out, but ultimately my two brothers said somebody needed to go, and their votes outnumbered my one. I sold out my share of the company that October, took a down payment, and it was set up such that the remainder of the payoff would be paid out over the next five years.

Problem solved? Time for a new beginning and a fresh restart on life? Not hardly. Even with the buyout, I was devastated. My whole life and dreams had been built around that company. It was a major step down in my life, a retreat back to a place where I didn't want to be. One thing hadn't changed, though: I continued to try to drink away my problems and feelings, becoming even more suicidal at times.

Dream House

When I was a teenager, I had been enamored by this nice big house that was being built out in the country on a large hill, the top of which provided a panoramic view from which you could see for miles. I never got that house completely out of my head and had long wished secretly that it would become mine someday. And that's exactly what happened. In the fall of '97, my wife and I bought the place. It came with ten acres, although it needed some sprucing up and cleaning by the time we took ownership of it. So we spent the next few years working and sweating to remodel the house and clean up the property, with my "severance package" (a fancy-sounding term that felt out of kilter with my settlement) from the company now owned solely by my brothers tiding us over.

At the same time, even with our house taking shape, our marriage was crumbling. Whatever it was that had drawn us together during our high school years and later after her divorce had disappeared, and now our emerging incompatibility, worsened by all the drinking, was tearing us apart. Many times I would tell her that I was going to kill myself. My grandpa had given me a Smith and Wesson .38 caliber revolver some years before, more as a favor to himself than as a gift of home defense to me.

Have Gun, Will Use It

My grandmother had been ill with Alzheimer's, and Grandpa would get depressed caring for her and missing the close companionship he had shared with her for decades. It was clear he had given me the gun in order to keep him from killing himself, not knowing what evil lurked with it now being in my possession. Giving it to me had possibly saved him, but it didn't belong in my hands either. From the first time that Grandpa put it in my hands, it hit me that someday I would be using it to end my own life. It was a dark cloud of a thought that took up occupancy in my head, and I was ill-equipped to get it out of there.

Sometimes, when I would get really drunk, I would put the barrel in my mouth and think for a long time about pulling the trigger, with a bullet loaded, of course. I remember one time driving out into our pasture late at night, and shooting the pistol into the ground to make Joanna think I had really done it. I can still see her walking all the way out there, eight months pregnant, not knowing if she would find me alive or my head blown off. It was sick imagery on my part and a poor attempt to get her attention.

We would argue and scream at each other. Lots of strife. We were never violent with each other, but many times a hole would get punched or kicked into a wall; at other times something would get destroyed. Here's the kicker (no pun intended): We had made an agreement before we got married that neither of us would ever go into a drinking establishment without the other accompanying him or her. The idea was that we would hold ourselves accountable to one another, making sure the other didn't drink too much and to avoid being separated from the other, as drinking while in the presence of available members of the opposite sex could very well create a temptation too powerful to pass up. But all it did, in sticking together like that, was make both of us even heavier drinkers and more likely to be at war with one another. Alcohol has an incredible ability to create problems out of thin air and made already-existent bad problems even worse.

"In essence, alcohol abuse causes a person to make drinking a priority," is how americanaddictioncenters.org puts it, offering a spot-on summation of alcoholism, a disease that I know so well. Here's what else they say on their website, uncanny to me in how it relates so closely to the issues I have dealt with over the years:

"As a result, the time, effort, and resources formerly dedicated to life-sustaining activities, such as working and spending time with the family, are disrupted. Initially, a person may think that abusing alcohol will help them deal with these stressors, but as they continue to drink a lot, over time, this abuse can turn into dependence on the substance. Once individuals become psychologically addicted, alcohol abuse can become all-consuming. As individuals are often part of social networks, it is easy to understand how alcohol abuse has a ripple effect across a person's entire network of family, friends, employers, colleagues, and anyone else who depends on the person."[4]

Not only that, we still drank a lot around our home. Oh, heck, yeah! One of my favorite pastimes was to load a cooler on my four-wheeler, and drive it all around our expansive property, stopping and having a beer every now and then, just sitting there enjoying it, or drinking while driving. *Yee-haw!!!* That's fun when your judgment is totally impaired, which mattered little to me. As long as I was smashed like that, my problems were on hiatus, only to come roaring back within hours. I also spent a lot of time drinking and driving in my truck, usually by myself. I also loved listening to that old country music, like Merle, Cash, and Waylon,

---

[4] Meredith Watkins, "Alcoholism and Family/Marital Problems," americanaddictioncenters.org, May 7, 2021, https://americanaddictioncenters.org/alcoholism-treatment/family-marital-problems, viewed May 31, 2021.

while drinking. What I didn't realize was that they were only songs, and I didn't have to try to live them out.

My marriage was crazy at times. My brother Steve asked me one time if I was trying to write my own country song, acting it out so I could use my own life as an inspiration to put it to lyrics and music, I suppose, sort of like people who watch movies, such as a James Bond spy thriller, imagining themselves being in that role and getting to travel to all those nice places, seducing all those beautiful women, and getting to kick butt in the most cunning and dramatic ways imaginable. Actually, now that I think about it, I have long had some of that James Bond DNA inside of me, although I almost always preferred a nice cold beer to a martini shaken not stirred. My family used to joke about me relating to the song, "Hank Williams, You Wrote My Life." That's a pretty accurate connection, actually, as was my nickname "Otis," named after the town drunk in Mayberry on *The Andy Griffith Show*. Andy's Otis would often show up at jail in a drunken stupor barely able to stand up, then lock himself into a jail cell so he would have some place comfortable to sleep it off. While I might have been an authentic drunk, along the lines of Otis, I really believed I loved my wife through it all. I never even considered cheating on her. Being born and raised in a Christian family, and with my dad being a Vietnam veteran, I was a strong supporter of our military and walking that line of discipline, and somehow managing to hold onto Christian values, even when it got to be really tough sledding.

Chicago, Here We Come

Except . . . there was this trip I took to Chicago with three friends of mine. One of them was going to jail in a few weeks (no, his name wasn't Otis), so we decided to treat him to a wild weekend before he got himself locked up.

We rented the penthouse suite at the Hyatt in downtown Chicago and used a limo to get around the Windy City all weekend, to include taking in some baseball. The first day we hit a White Sox game, and then later a Cubs game—that's the nice thing about being in a city with two Major League Baseball teams. If one team is out of town on a road trip, chances are at least fifty-fifty the other team will be in town, and few ballparks are as fun to take in a game as cozy Wrigley Field, home to the Cubbies.

Of course we stayed drunk the whole time, and went through thousands of dollars. On the second day, we went to another Sox game. Then things started to get crazy. Three of the four of us were married, with the exception being the one about to go up the river to serve his sentence. Later that night, we ended up hitting gentleman's clubs around town, with plenty of beautiful female skin on display, not to mention all the booze. One of my friends vomited in the limo, and we eventually made it back to our penthouse suite, severely intoxicated. Unbeknownst to me, one of my friends, who was married but had a habit of cheating on his wife, had called and arranged for prostitutes to come by.

I ended up passed out drunk on my bed and assumed everyone else was also going to hit the hay, too. At four in the morning, I woke up with a naked prostitute in bed with me, touching me and just generally holding my attention and lighting my fuse. What else could I do in such a weakened, distorted sense of consciousness? Being severely drunk and disillusioned, I had made a wrong decision that changed my life forever. I can still remember the next morning (after the sun was up, that is), and how I felt—hungover and ashamed, with tremendous guilt. I was looking down on downtown Chicago from the top of the Hyatt. It was a beautiful sight, but all I could think about was what I had done. Sure, the chances of Joanna ever finding out were slim, but that didn't matter. I knew what I had done, and I would have to live with it. At that time, I thought less of myself than I ever had. I hated and resented the fact that I drank like I did, but I knew I was an alcoholic and would have to either get help or live with it. I chose to live with it, always thinking that I would be able to control it someday.

I recently found some letters my mom gave me—that's what parents do as they get older. She gave me letters she had kept that I had written while I was traveling, like when I first went to New Mexico. I always signed them, "God Bless." It surprised me a little bit to see that I had done that—I had totally forgotten. Even in my drunkenness, my depression, my failed marriage, and everything else, I've always been hard core when it comes to knowing right and wrong. I'm one of the most dedicated people. I would never go out with a friend's girlfriend. I had standards, with work as well as my personal life. I'm not joking.

An Honest Life's Work

When we started our business, my brothers and I swore we were going to do it honestly. We weren't going to cheat anybody. Here in the business world, especially in our business world, it's easy to take people, to con them, to scam them out of large amounts of money. In our business, if you really wanted to, you could take from trusting folks thousands and thousands of dollars here and there, and we decided we weren't going to do that. Even with all my mistakes and all the bad things I did, I was raised to tell right from wrong. The bad things I did were almost always tied in to my alcohol abuse. I didn't do things like that when I was sober.

Have you ever seen the movie *Eight Seconds?* There's a part in that movie where the lead character, a champion bull rider played by Luke Perry, breaks down and tells his wife he cheated on her. Joanna and I were watching that movie and I was about half blitzed. Naturally, I got overwhelmed by watching it and I told her what had happened in Chicago. It had been a couple of months. I told her and said, "I don't blame you if you want to leave me," and I got in the truck and left. I didn't give her a chance to say a whole lot. She was kind of in shock. She called me on my cell phone and said to come home, that we would work this out. That was pretty much the end of it. There were no repercussions. I didn't hang out with the same friends too much anymore.

We moved on from there, but the booze and verbal abuse continued, back and forth. I was never violently abusive, but verbally abusive, no question. Many times throughout the years, I had tried to stop drinking, with no luck. Sometimes I would make it a week or two, and sometimes I couldn't make it through a day. I remember my mother asking me to get help after one of my worst drunks. She said, "Just twenty-eight days in rehab, that's it." So, to prove a point, I went twenty-eight days without drinking, then got drunk on the twenty-ninth. My parents were just as frustrated with my drinking as everyone else.

Here Come the Kids and the Family Business

Our first daughter, Courtney, was born in 1998, and our second, Grace, arrived in 2000. Even as bad as I was, I always felt dedicated to my daughters. I took them with me to jobsites whenever it was convenient. I always had time for them, and loved spending every minute I could with them. They were definitely spoiled, due to the fact that we were able to buy them anything and everything.

In 1999, my wife and I started another tower company. Just like with my previous company, things went really well, kicking into gear quickly. We were making a lot of money, and I was spending it as fast as we made it. We had several employees, and we were making hundreds of thousands of dollars a year, and that was in addition to what I was receiving from my two brothers in terms of buyout money.

Looking back, if had played my cards right (which I didn't), I could have retired around age thirty. The first big investment we made—actually, the blame goes solely on me—was buying forty-five acres that surrounded our ten-acre farm. We really didn't need any more property, but due to my unchecked pride, we ended up with it anyway. It was like a big game of Monopoly to me, almost like I was playing with phony money, now that was I was in possession of a good chunk of it.

My pride factor concerned a neighbor of ours with whom we did not get along. He didn't like us, and we made it clear to him that the personal animosity was mutual. There were fifty-seven acres situated between our respective properties, which our neighbor wanted badly, but he couldn't come to terms with the owner. After an argument with this guy one Sunday afternoon, I decided I would "show him." I called the owner and asked how much he was asking. He gave me a ridiculous price, and without hesitation, I said okay. He came to our house that same evening, we signed a purchase agreement, and I gave him a check to cover the deposit. So, I got the ample acreage, even though I didn't need it. It was a beautiful property, though, in that thirty of those fifty-seven acres—just over half—were nicely wooded. Tons of healthy trees. I had it select-cut for timber for the next year, and cut a whole lot of it the next year to sell to help cover financial problems we had run into—with reckless me at the steering wheel.

There was another time when one of my employees and I were out drinking and driving around one afternoon, and I managed to make another astute decision to buy another large piece of property. Couldn't help myself. We had stopped at the local convenience store to buy fuel and pick up a few things when I noticed an auction flyer in the window. It was for fifty-six acres about ten miles away. I thought, *I should buy that.* I then noticed the date and time, and realized the auction was that very night, only a couple of hours away. So I called my wife and told her to contact the auction company and ask how much we needed to put down. They told her what was needed. I then asked her to hurry to the bank and get a cashier's check, which she did and I met her back at the house. The three of us went to this auction in the next little town down the road, by which time I was pretty well lit. We had been drinking for hours, meaning there's no way I should have been buying anything. Needless to say, before the night was over, I had spent the money and bought the property. We now had 168 acres of property that we didn't need.

This is as good a time as any to go back to americanaddiction-centers.org for some added insight on alcohol's destructive role in my life. They could have had me in mind when they wrote this:

"Alcohol is not free. Although even the strictest accountant or budgeter will make an allowance for entertainment expenses, ongoing drinking can quickly cause people to spend beyond their allotment for socializing. It is well established that alcohol abuse can lead to serious financial problems, but not only because of the actual money spent on alcohol.

"Because your inhibitions are lowered when you drink alcohol, you may be more likely to impulsively buy things without thinking through the consequences of those purchases in the moment."[5]

Spending money was never a problem for me. I had nice tractors and all the right equipment to go with them. Whenever I needed a certain tool or other equipment, I bought it. Then there were my toys. I had several four-wheelers, a ski boat, and whatever else I wanted. I remember buying a new four-wheeler that had just came on the market. A few days later I decided I would test it during one of my drunken stupors. I took it out to an old coal mine with some other guys. The first thing I did was

---

[5] Meredith Watkins, "Alcoholism and Family/Marital Problems."

try to climb a steep hill. The four-wheeler flipped backward, and I rolled off the back. Somehow, the several-hundred-pound ATV went right over the top of me and landed upright, still running. I hurt my leg, but that was all. I easily could have been crushed, paralyzed, or even killed. I guess it was another time that God had me covered.

Because my new ATV was damaged, and I had to wait to get it fixed, I just bought another one, even more expensive. I believe at one time I had six different ATVs. I even bought one for my daughter, Courtney, when she was only two. Many times I would be riding a four-wheeler drunk, running it sixty or seventy miles per hour down the road or across a field. I had bought special racks for them that would hold a large cooler full of beer. I never went anywhere without my beer, especially playing on my toys.

There were many times during a drinking binge that I would become suicidal, which I have talked about earlier. On another such occasion, after another long argument with Joanna, I decided I would end it. I can still see myself sitting at the top of the stairs with my revolver in my mouth. My wife walked out of the bedroom, jumped backed a few feet, then pulled the gun out and hid it from me. After that, I went out to the barn and took off on another of my many four-wheeler jaunts, with it now being in the middle of the night. I don't really remember much from there, other that waking up in the barn before morning. My older brother always told me that I had a death wish, and if I kept playing with fire, I would get burned.

One warm May evening, my brothers had invited over to one of their houses to spend some time chilling around a fire. I had been drinking all day, and ended up feeling suicidal later that night. My wife had both girls in the bathtub when I took off. Joanna had no idea what I was up to. I then proceeded to swallow a whole bottle of sleeping pills, and kept drinking and driving, eventually showing up at my brother's place. When I got out of the truck, he asked what was wrong with my eyes. That was the last thing I remembered. I guess I passed out cold. I'm a big guy, and it took everything my brothers had to load me in my truck and drive me ten miles to the hospital. They didn't know what was wrong or what I had taken, and they couldn't take a chance on waiting for an ambulance. My sister-in-law called my wife, and told her I was on my way to the hospital. When they got me there, they immediately pumped my stomach and put a catheter in. Sometime the next afternoon I finally woke up, with my wife beside me. I had no idea where I was or why or how I got there. They had me strapped down with oxygen going into my nose. I proceeded to check myself out and head home. Again, I decided to try and stay sober, but after a few weeks without drinking, I gave in to the cravings and was right back at it.

Although I was a hard-core alcoholic—and on occasion not a very nice guy to my wife and others, there was a good side of me that came out once in a while. There were times when I sponsored youth baseball teams, and even chartered a motor coach to a big league game a couple times for the team and their parents. I've always had a love of children, and would do anything I could to help out a kid. I carried bubble gum in my truck, and several kids around town knew where it was and helped themselves. When the carnival came to town every year, I would buy ride bracelets for all the kids in the county on public assistance. I donated to various school activities and sponsored field trips. I went to youth football, baseball, and basketball games to support some of the kids I knew. I had a few elderly friends as well as family, and spent time with them whenever possible. I feel like I was a good neighbor and helped out whenever they needed anything.

Then there were the veterans. I've always been a major supporter of our vets. I started taking my girls to veterans programs before they had a clue what it was. I had made trips to the VA hospital to give rides to veterans who didn't have a way to get to where they wanted to go. I was even into politics. I actually ran for county council one time, and didn't have a clue what I was doing. I stayed drunk for most of the campaign, and somehow only lost by twelve votes. Thank God I didn't win. That was the last thing I needed.

My marriage wasn't always bad, either. I believe she and I did love each other, but too many of my issues, along with a few other people's problems, put things in turmoil. We traveled some, went to a few concerts, and, of course, spent time with our beautiful daughters, Courtney and Grace.

I can remember the two of us, Joanna and me, lying together during the middle of the night in a field of clover out in front of our house. We were just staring at the moon, listening to crickets and frogs from a nearby pond, and we were talking, laughing, and, of course, crying. It was almost like we both knew that our dream life wasn't meant to be, and someday it would all come to an end. I had been given everything I dreamed of: a successful business, marriage to my high school sweetheart, purchase of my dream home and farm, and, of course, the birth and presence of our two angels from God. Yes, I had everything—everything but a relationship with God.

I had become so successful, and so arrogant, that I cussed God, and swore I didn't need him. I had completely forgotten about the Christian life in which I grew up. Between the booze, a crumbling marriage, and years of fighting depression, I just didn't think God existed for me. Looking back, it was obvious that he did, or I definitely wouldn't be telling this story.

6

Drunk, Bankrupt & Divorced

JOANNA HAD TWO NAMES FOR ME. One was Michael—that's me, obviously. The other guy wearing my body was named "Miguel." He had a completely different persona from Michael's. There you have it: I had two personalities, and they could switch in a blink of an eye. My wife told me there had to be something else going on with me separate from the drinking, because of my mood swings and so forth. Alcohol is a depressant, and for someone who is already suffering from depression, drinking can only exacerbate the problem. It doesn't take a psychologist or psychiatrist to figure that one out.

The good side of me was fun-loving and happy; I was nice to people and good to them, always lending a helping hand and, in her case, treating her well, like a woman should be treated by her husband. When it came to the bad side, I would turn mean and verbally abusive, although not physically abusive; I've never been physically abusive to a woman. However, I would break things. Or I would grab a gun and go start shooting at things to let off steam. Anything I could shoot, I'd shoot. I would get mean when I would get down, and I would become suicidal. And I would make decisions that I shouldn't make. Like firing my employees in another one of my angry outbursts out of nowhere.

I remember the day. It was a Monday—June 11, 2001. Exactly three months before the 9/11 attacks on America. I had come off my medicines—antidepressants. Over the weekend, on Sunday actually, the day before, the crew had hung out at my place to have some fun. Nothing unusual about that. It was a fun place to hang out even when they weren't working there. I had two ponds, one with a zipline off of it. Plus we had all kinds of four-wheelers, and we'd shoot guns. But on that Sunday, I got in a disagreement with some of them over something stupid, and my anger quickly spread around to everybody. I was in one of those moods, abetted by plenty of alcohol, and I was crashing.

The next morning, on Monday, they all showed up at my house like they did every morning, as if nothing had changed. Whatever had happened Sunday was over as far as they were concerned. A fresh start for another work week beckoned. They all had come into the house and were just sitting around, when I walked in and said they were all fired, "See ya!" Obviously, a night's sleep hadn't fixed me.

My wife and I worked out of the house and I had a shop that was outside, separate from the house. On a typical work day we'd sit there and go over what we were going to do for the day. Except this time I came downstairs from my bedroom and sternly told my working crew they were out of a job. Well, duh, they were in shock. Who could blame them? On top of that, they were half-scared of me because they knew I had guns all over the place and how crazy I could be—they weren't going to argue with me. They just started walking. They didn't have any vehicles of their own—they had showed up in a company truck—and I let them keep on walking. There were about six of them. We lived out in the middle of nowhere. I assumed they eventually managed to get to a phone and call someone to come pick them up and take them home. I certainly wasn't going to chauffeur them.

It had been about three years or so since I had sold out to my brothers and was now working a company of my own, with my wife helping me. We were really doing well, making more money than I had been making with my brothers, doing the same stuff, putting up towers. Sometimes we were competing against my brothers on projects, and other times we would work together on projects, or they would just hand one off to me. To this day we still do business together at times. We were also starting up more companies; at one time between us we had six different corporations (two tower construction companies, one steel fabrication company, one telecom system leasing company and two tower-leasing companies). Business was good and things were rolling, despite my recklessness of mind and emotions. It seems like everything I touched turned to gold back then, and I couldn't really explain why. It seemed my business sense was just dead on. My wife did all the bookkeeping, I made all the decisions, and things just kept rolling. I was able to make all this happen without ever going to business school or college of any sort.

It was during this time when things were going well with the businesses that I bought those fifty-seven or so acres that the neighbor we didn't like had been trying to buy for himself. I ended up paying $122,000 for it, the first part of it being the $30,000 down payment. That was about twenty years ago, and today the property would be worth about twice that—around a quarter of a million dollars. It had some great soil, with about half that property tillable and the other half wooded.

Back then that neighbor guy was kind of a bully. I would say nobody liked him, but chances are he had at least one or two in his family who tolerated him. I sure didn't. I knew he had a lot of money in a local sawmill and was old enough to be my dad, making him about the same age as my mom as well. Here I was a thirty-year-old thinking I could compete with him, only to find out I couldn't.

After it was all said and done—after I had gotten divorced and gone bankrupt and all that—he bought all my property including my house—the dream house I had longed for all those years. Funny, though, how things change over time. That man and I have actually gotten along for years now. He became a Christian a few years ago, by which time I had turned around my own life. I actually like him. But at that point in my life, around 2001, I didn't care much for him, and it was mutual.

Bankruptcy

Despite all the success I was having in business, the never-ending spending and drinking was dragging us down financially. We filed for bankruptcy about a year before our divorce, and it took another year post-divorce before it was settled. One very important lesson I learned in this is that banks are not there for you. They are out to get whatever they can. If you get into any sort of arrangement with a bank, such as with a business loan, you might think they are your friends, but they are not. Sure, you might have gabbed a lot in getting to know the loan officer—maybe it's even somebody you often see in church or have beers with from time to time—but trust me when I say they are not really your friend. I'm not saying they are bad people or scammers, they are just in it to make a buck. After all, they are a bank, and a bank is all about money—making it, saving it, investing it, and nobody should ever dare getting in their way.

What took so long with our bankruptcy were the properties tied up in it. The bank was fighting the trustee for whatever equity was in the property—the amount of its valuation over what had been put into it in buying it (with most if it being paid through debt service, by me). There was equity in it, but the bank didn't want us to have the equity, and the trustee wanted the equity that the bank claimed belonged to it. It was a mess.

Even with the bankruptcy, my wife and I had a lot of equity. When I was buying property, I'd put down 10 or 20 percent or so, such that if I was buying a $100,000 property I would already have at least $10,000-20,000 equity in it. With bankruptcy in the works, all we wanted was to sell our properties and pay off the debt, keeping the equity for ourselves, but the bank wasn't going to let us do that. They wanted our equity, period. And there was more than one bank involved. We had a couple lines of credits for our businesses, and the banks that held those lines of credit were fighting against the bank that had our mortgage. That's why it took two years to settle it. There was nothing left from the property or the house for us when it was all done, except I kept the towers through the bankruptcy. That's because one of the businesses I had with my brothers owned the communication towers, which were not part of any collateral that had been put up to secure any of the loans or lines of credit.

We filed for Chapter 13 bankruptcy, which, as described at experian.com, is "also known as a reorganization bankruptcy, gives you the chance to keep your property (including secured assets like your home and car) if you successfully complete a court-mandated repayment plan that lasts between three and five years."[6]

We had an attorney, a young guy I had known years before. He hadn't been practicing very long and was absolutely terrible.

---

[6] Hillary Back, "What Is the Difference Between Chapter 7 and Chapter 13 Bankruptcy?", experian.com, April 7, 2021, https://www.experian.com/blogs/ask-experian/bankruptcy-chapter-7-vs-chapter-13/, viewed June 2, 2021.

We had so much involved with so many different accounts and properties that he was in way over his head; he couldn't handle it. Even the trustee for the bankruptcy told us that our attorney wasn't any good, but we were stuck. We couldn't get a different attorney. We had already paid him. We had to stick with what we had.

I had been divorced and moved away by the time we got everything settled. What had happened was that we had gotten behind on some of the payments. The guy at the bank handling our loan came to us and said they were going to foreclose, but offered us an out by saying that if we paid something like ten thousand dollars, he could cancel the foreclosure. We paid it, but the bank continued into the foreclosure anyway. The guy had outright lied to us.

Each of our properties was secured separately, which meant we could sell a couple of them and be fine. Then the banker called us one day and said, "We can save you some money," and this was during the foreclosure. He said they could redo the loan in such a way that, "I can save you a couple of hundred a month," which seemed kind of crazy, but I didn't know any better—I was drunk most of the time. I went ahead and signed over one of the loans for a longer term and cheaper interest, at which point he did some fancy paperwork and tied all the properties together into one loan. And because of that, we couldn't sell just one property to help ourselves out financially.

We had been bamboozled. This guy, unlike our bozo of an attorney, knew what he was doing, and I'm sure his superiors were pushing him. The federal trustee told us that the bank we were dealing with was the most corrupt bank he'd ever dealt with. And here it was a bank I'd been doing business with since I was a teenager. The banker was a childhood friend of my wife's, as well as a childhood friend of mine. In his defense, he did what he thought he had to do, and my wife and I were both drunk and we didn't know what we were doing. They took full advantage of us.

I know it now: If I hadn't been a drunk, I wouldn't have been taken advantage of. That would never happen to me today. A banker will never again take advantage of me, as I'm too well-versed in banking and how it works. I'm very careful about everything I do—where I do business, with whom I do business, and so forth. But when you are drunk all the time, you just trust everybody. You don't know the difference. That was in 2002, and throughout that summer we tried to save what we had.

Based on the terms of the Chapter 13, our payments had been set at eleven or twelve thousand dollars a month. There was no way we could have paid them, and now everything was bundled together, without the flexibility for my wife and me to sell any one of the properties separately. We had a half million dollars in assets and a half million dollars in debt, and we had been trying to keep our house and our properties without filing bankruptcy. Fat chance, as it turns out. Because a Chapter 13 allows you to reorganize and pay your debt over a long period of time, it takes a little bit of the pressure off. It can work for certain situations, but it has to start with a husband and wife who have a solid relationship, are sober, and are responsible human beings when it comes to managing their personal and professional lives. We struck out on all counts.

Our marriage was continually spiraling downward, made worse by the stress of the bankruptcy and the fact we were drinking all the time—both of us. We were going out to drink and also drinking at home. We even started running with a different group of people, tossing our standards to the wayside. The people we were hanging around with were basically low, white trash; they cheated on each other and slept around. We just stayed as drunk as we could most of the time.

By Christmas of that year, 2002, we knew it was over for us. Until then, I had never thought we would ever separate. Even with all the pressure of the bankruptcy accompanied by the marriage strife, I don't believe I ever thought we would get divorced. I guess I was just naïve. Once in a great while we would go to church, and it was always in my heart to be a Christian. I always wanted that. My wife and were married by a justice of the peace, but I never stopped thinking about eventually having a church ceremony. We talked about it, but we never made it that far. It was just something that kept hanging around out there. I did go to church occasionally, but not a whole lot.

I ended that year in a crazy mode. I'd been traveling a lot, and that got me to thinking she had started running around on me. She never did like my business. She liked the money I was making, but she didn't like it when I took chances and the way I got it. I was a risk taker, probably still am. For one thing, I invested in stocks. The stock market was booming back in the late nineties, so I sunk some money into stocks or property. I'd buy this or that. I spent money like it was going out of style. We made it through Christmas, although we were pretty much broke. She would end up crying, a lot, and my brother's wife would have to come over to pick up Courtney and Grace to take care of them for a while. I believe Joanna was on edge as much as I was.

Last Dance

It was sometime after Christmas that I came back home off the road, and that's when everything happened. I had just driven ten hours straight through from Minneapolis, and I remember thinking about where I was and what my life had become. I was physically sick, mentally sick, financially broke, discouraged. I just broke down crying while still driving. I cried out and started praying to God, telling him, "I know I gave up on you. I ran from you and said I didn't need you, and you weren't part of my life. God, I need you now, if you're still there for me and still care for me. I can't live this way anymore."

I think it was Tuesday when I left for Minneapolis, and her birthday was going to be the following Sunday. We always threw big parties for her birthday. She didn't think I was going to make it back for it this time, and for a while I didn't think so, either, because of the extent of the job I had up in Minneapolis. I worked extra-long hours just so I could get it done several days ahead of time and make it back in time for the birthday party. When I got home, the first thing I saw was two teenage girls babysitting the kids, and everyone was shocked to see me. That was weird, and I knew my wife was out somewhere at her birthday party. But the babysitters had been told to stay all night. I headed out to go to the party but not before telling the girls I would be coming back home, that night, to be with my kids.

My wife was in shock when I showed up there. We danced, and I asked the band to play "Wonderful Tonight." My parents were there, too. It got late and I wanted to go check on our kids. And she said, "Well, I'm not going home. It's my party and I'm staying." So I started out the door, and that's when she came up behind me and hit me in the back of the head with her hand. I turned around and just looked at her for a while, then I went home. I told the teenage girls they could go home now. They said they were supposed to stay all night. I said, "No, you're not supposed to stay all night. These are my kids. This is my house. You're leaving." So they left.

I think this sort of thing had been going on for some time. The girls were quite close to her, and I assumed she had been buying beer and stuff for them. The next morning I woke up and my wife still wasn't there. She never came home. It was now Sunday, her birthday. After two days of her not coming home, I went to the courthouse to pick up divorce papers. There happened to be a young woman working there with whom I had gone to school. She informed me that my wife had come by the day before to get a restraining order on me. I said, "That's kind of weird. I never hurt her or anything like that, ever." That prompted me to go right ahead and file for divorce, and I filled out the paperwork myself. A woman working at my brother's office notarized it for me, and I turned it in.

That started a war. I was told that the restraining order she slapped on me was not an uncommon thing for women to do. So I went and got an attorney for myself. Now we both had attorneys. I guess this is where we stick our tongues out at each other.

When we went to court, the judge said he wouldn't hear the case because of my family—everyone in town, including him, knew my family—so he recused himself from the case. It was going to be another month or so before we could get back into a court because it was going to have to go through a county court, down the road. My attorney agreed with her attorney to let her see the girls. She needed the permission because I now had possession of the house, because she had left it and was now staying with her drinking friends. I would take them to daycare in the morning, and then my wife would pick them up at daycare and spend the day with them—but she had to have them back by four o'clock. I would come and get them and take them home. I had custody of the girls; they were with me. Possession is nine-tenths of the law. The girls were four and two. After about two weeks of that, I finally couldn't take it anymore.

After being home from rehab for about a month, I went to stay with my parents, while my wife and the girls were living at our house. At one point we actually talked about getting back together and here I was, now two months sober. She was still drinking. I said, "I am trying to get sober, and I can't get back together with you if you're still drinking. There's nothing I want more than to keep my family together."

After we got divorced, I never knew whom the girls were with when my ex had custody. I didn't want to get back together with her because she wouldn't quit drinking. I went to AA—Alcoholics Anonymous—a lot and I had a sponsor. I also started working for my brother. I wasn't in physical pain anymore. When I started working for my brother and traveling, I had to stay in a hotel room with somebody else. They might be drinking, and here I was fresh in sobriety rooming with somebody who's drinking. I think when I was done, I was done. There were local restaurant/bars I'd go to with my friends, and they would sit in there and drink, and I would drink iced tea. On other occasions I could go to a bar with my buddies, shoot pool, and not even think about drinking. I eventually rented a little house and the girls were with me a lot. My wife liked to go out and party, so I had the girls anytime I wanted.

Courtney was four at this time, just old enough to have a pretty good sense of things. Nearly twenty years later, she remembers how she perceived what was going on between me and my soon-to-be ex-wife. Ask me to remember what I can from age four, and I pretty much draw a blank. Courtney is light years ahead of me in that regard.

"They got divorced when I was about four," says Courtney, who was interviewed for this book by someone other than me, knowing she could be more open and objective speaking to someone else. "I kind of blocked out a lot of childhood memories from about the age of four or five. But once my dad got custody, it was like they'd drop us off with each other and not talk to each other at all. So, I was always kind of like the middleman. If one of them wanted to tell the other one something, they'd tell me to tell them. To this day, they still have a little bit of hatred toward each other.

And they hardly ever talk to one another unless it's like an emergency, like, hell's freezing over or something.

"It definitely wasn't a good thing. It was a little bit stressful for me. It was just a constant back and forth. Either they couldn't get along when they did talk, or they would just refuse to talk to each other. I had to listen to each one of them bicker about the other one when I was relaying messages. I'd have to kind of remind each parent, like, 'You're supposed to co-parent here. Like, leave me out of it.'"

Then there were our ongoing financial issues, which hadn't gone on hiatus. Now we were on to Chapter 7 bankruptcy, which meant we pretty much lost everything we had as far as our material life. We lost our properties, we lost our vehicles, and we lost our house. Pretty much anything we had that was worth anything we lost. We could have petitioned to keep this and that, but it wasn't worth it. It was time to get out of it. As for the divorce, they weren't going to give me custody. So she and I settled the divorce out of court. We still had our attorney, but we went around our house, our property, and our farm with a notepad and worked it out between us what each of us would get. We created our respective lists and gave them to the attorney. Our divorce was drawn up, we each signed the papers, and that was it.

I didn't want her to push the custody issue, considering that I had already tried to kill myself and knew I didn't have solid ground to stand on. And when it comes to custody issues and children, it's definitely a woman's world. She ended up with full custody, and I only had visitation. That wasn't fair by any stretch, but the law favored her. In the twenty-first century, it still is true that, generally, a woman performing the same job as a man doesn't get paid as much as the man, but flip it around and women still have a big edge when it comes to divorce and custody of any dependent children. But you rarely hear about that flip side—our "woke" culture hasn't managed to get to that one yet. During the whole five years that she had custody, however, I was able to keep Courtney and Grace with me anytime I wanted. If I wasn't in town, she'd have to pay a babysitter in order to do what she was doing, which gave me the opening to have our two girls pretty much anytime I wanted.

My ex lived in welfare housing down in the projects with the kids. She was a regular June Cleaver (sarcasm). I tried a couple of times to get custody, but without success. At the time I was working for my younger brother, Tony, and was often traveling to jobs. Anytime I was in town, I had the girls. Even then, I was still having issues of my own, experiencing breakdowns and panic attacks. It had been more than a year since I had quit drinking, and I was still experiencing withdrawal symptoms. The day of my suicide attempt, February 5, 2003, was the last time I took a drink.

It was a pretty rough time for me. I still had depression, and it felt all the time like I had gotten hit by a bus. I went to all kind of doctors and psychiatrists while they tried to figure out what kind of medicine to put me on. Nothing seemed to work. Meanwhile, I was trying to pay off debts to people we'd known personally. My wife had been running up a bill with the daycare provider that I didn't know about. Once we got divorced, I found out that the daycare debt had reached four thousand dollars. My wife didn't even work during this time, and yet she would take the kids to daycare when I was out on the road. Then she would go spend her time doing whatever she wanted to do. I ended up having to pay back a lot of debt, such as to the daycare and her insurance. People I personally knew were owed money by her, and I ended up paying them, too. It took me a long time, two or three years, to get everything paid off. I didn't want to put all that into bankruptcy, so I paid them off personally.

Elvis Got the Ring

One thing about my divorce still makes me smile—how I ended up giving away my wedding band. It's a story I still like to tell folks, and it usually gets a good chuckle—out of them as well as out of me.

It was an original, a nice wedding band with a diamond in it and really done up nice. When I bought it new, it cost me something like thirty-five hundred dollars. I carried it with me for a couple years beyond the divorce, more from the standpoint of not wanting to let go of a good piece of jewelry vs. my trying to hold on to a piece of my marriage. That was gone for good, and good riddance.

I kept it in the console of my truck as I traveled around doing jobs, not ever really knowing what to do with it, except to look at it every now and then to admire the diamond and the other nice shiny decorative things on it. I'd bought my ex different pieces of jewelry over the years, and she said she was going to give all her wedding stuff to our daughters (as far as I know, she never did that). Well, with our not having any sons, I wasn't sure what to do with the wedding band, until it came to me one time while I was driving out of Atlanta, heading north. I was somewhere around Chattanooga when I see this guy on an exit ramp thumbing for a ride. As I got up to him, he gave me one of those "C'mon, man" looks, as if he were pleading.

If I don't have my kids with me while driving, I often pick up people to give them a ride and, to be honest, I enjoy the company, at least for a little while. It can get pretty dull and lonely out there on the road, even with Hank, Merle, and the rest of the boys pouring out their hearts inside my truck. And I'm never too worried about picking up some bad dude along the way—I'm a pretty big dude still in decent enough shape to handle myself, and, like Paladin, I *Have Gun, Will Travel.*

So I pulled over, stopped, and let this guy in, and it turns out that he's an Elvis impersonator. Suddenly, the story gets better. He was headed to Nashville for the National Elvis Impersonator Convention, or whatever it's called. I guess this is actually a thing. Elvis impersonators come from all over the world to go to this convention. As we headed up the road toward Nashville, he told me all about this Elvis event and how it worked. At one point, he said, "Oh, yeah, I've also got some songs." Then he mentions how he has a friend of a friend of a friend in Nashville who was going to help him get these songs recorded or something like that. He didn't really have much on him, including money.

As we approached Nashville, I pulled off I-24 at La Vergne, Tennessee, about twenty miles southeast of Nashville, at one of those Pilot truck stops. He told me that was as good a place as any to let him out, my assumption being he was going to have someone come pick him up, or maybe he was going to grab a cheap motel room somewhere around there.

As he started to get out of my truck, I got to thinking he could use a little help, and I thought of the wedding band stashed in my console. I said, "Bud, I ain't got any cash," but I reached into my console and pulled out the wedding band and gave it to him, saying, "Here, take this." He opened it up (it was still in the small box it came in) and he said, "My gosh, I'll treasure this forever."

"No, you won't," I said. "You'll go sell the dang thing and take the money and do what you need to do with it. You don't have to treasure it."

"Oh, man. I thank you," he said, and then we said our farewells.

So that's my story—I gave away my wedding band to Elvis. I just thought you might enjoy this story before you turn the page and continue reading about my years-long struggle to win custody of our two daughters, Not much to smile about there, but I need to take you through it, nonetheless. You need to hear the whole sordid story to get a better picture of what I went through, what I put myself through, and how God got me through all of it toward a changed life, one I now live for his glory.

7
My Battle of Armageddon

BECAUSE I AM A CHRISTIAN, I acknowledge I am a flawed person who is a sinner. I know that the consequences of sin can be separation from God and even death. It is only through the blood-bought salvation of Jesus Christ that I have a path to eternity in Heaven. Left to my own devices without an embrace of and relationship to Christ, I have no hope. My drunkenness was a sin—not a popular conclusion to anyone content with their place in the secular world without a true relationship with God—but, to me, my years of sinning are indisputable. It is only through Jesus Christ that I now have a victorious life worth living.

I sure as heck have walked through hell to get to where I am, and I still take occasional forays close to that territory because I am a sinful man. All Christians bear that burden of sin. As we know from the Bible, at least those of us who read from it and have heard from it, the Apostle Paul, in addressing sin, told believers in Galatia that "For the flesh desires what is contrary to the Spirit, and the Spirit what is contrary to the flesh. They are in conflict with each other, so that you are not to do whatever you want." (Gal. 5:17, NIV). A couple verses later, Paul nails it on the head for me, essentially proclaiming that those of us who live a life of debauchery and sin sow the seeds of destruction in their present-day life. They forfeit any hope of an eternal life in Heaven. In a nutshell, man reaps what he sows.

Living through an attempted suicide by gunshot to my head didn't end my problems. Nor did my getting divorced from Joanna set me on a clear path to happiness and contentment. My stroll through hell on earth was far from over, a fate that is believable to anyone who has gone through a custody battle, whether during a divorce or post-divorce, and mine lasted for several years. If there is a purgatory on this planet, a custody fight with your ex-spouse over the children has to rank really high on the list. Especially when your ex has been granted primary custody of two children of preschool age even while she's ditching most of her parenting responsibilities while running around at all hours of the day and night, all while being unemployed. You're right: life is not fair. And being a Christian does not exempt you from that reality. But I believe it is only through Christ that you can persevere and overcome. I'd like to believe that's exactly what I've done. So far.

One key thing about a twelve-step program, at least the one I've been a part of for eighteen years, as of this writing, is that you're not supposed to make any major decisions for a year from the time you join the program. For me, workwise, that meant staying close to home in Indiana as of my base of operations, although I did travel a fair amount to continue doing my work. I had to—I had to go to where the work was, it wasn't going to come to me. After about a year so, I stepped out and contacted TerraCom, a tower company based in Atlanta for whom I had done some contracts in the past. I found out they were setting up a different division of the company, known as Lighthouse Tower, and they offered me the chance to come to Atlanta to run it. I jumped at it. At that time, my ex was dating a guy I actually liked and who used to be a friend. I thought things were going pretty good here, compared to how they had been, and she finally had herself a guy who could do her some good.

I packed up what little I had, a few pieces of furniture and some personal stuff, and then gave the rest to charity and local missions, and then I was out of there. I bought a brand-new truck, a Ford F150. With that and three plastic totes containing everything I owned, I left for Atlanta. I was starting over. Gone were the dream house, the properties, and all the work equipment and four-wheelers . . . you name it.

I got to Atlanta in April 2004, and right away the work was going really well. I liked my job, a lot. I ended up renting a big, beautiful, two-story house in a nice subdivision. I also had the girls for seven weeks that summer—just short of two months. My mom came with them to help me take care of them while I was working. Courtney was six and Grace four, by then. When I wasn't working, I would do stuff with them, like heading down to Florida to hit the beaches and do other things.

Things were good for me in Atlanta, and the girls enjoyed it, especially because they were with me. I know that sounds like I'm patting myself on the back, but I say this solely based on how much the girls enjoyed being with me and detested it whenever I had to return them to their mother. The difference was plainly evident. Night and day, or I should say, day and night. I had to take them back because I didn't have custody of them. One of the hardest things I ever did was taking them back to their "home" in Indiana, about an eight-hour drive.

Even though I was based in Atlanta, I was still traveling. It was still the nature of my work—I went wherever towers had to be built and erected. I don't remember all the details of those travels, but I'm pretty sure I was somewhere on the East Coast most of that time. Every chance I got, I would drive back to Indiana to see or pick up my girls for a stint—also to see my parents and my brothers. When I'd leave to head back out on work or straight to Atlanta, they would cry because life was not good for them in Indiana.

When I took them back to Indiana from that summer stay in Atlanta, my ex had already broken up with that guy I knew and liked, and she was dating somebody else. Even when I was away, I felt the sting of what was going on in Indiana, hundreds of miles away. One night in Atlanta, I got a call at one o'clock in the morning from an acquaintance telling me that my four-year-old daughter, Grace, was sleeping on a barstool at the Moose lodge. I asked the guy calling me to please call the police and report it. He told me it wouldn't do any good because the chief of police was already at the lodge as well as the mayor, both drinking and having a good time.

I knew it was bad because when I did go back to visit, their mother would have to hold them back so I could get in the truck without them grabbing me to either stay or jump into the truck with me, and they would scream and cry. I did some of that myself. It was gut-wrenching, and it showed just how wrong and borderline criminal it had been for the judge to have created this situation by giving her custody of the girls. It was excruciating for me to have to leave them. But I had to work.

On top of that, I never really wanted to go back to Indiana except to see my girls and family. That's where all my skeletons were, as well as the roots for some bad memories. It's amazing, though—God's work, actually—how a year's passage can change a man's heart. After almost a year, I felt God leading me back to Indiana to take care of my kids. By then I was going to church regularly and was pretty active in it. I was a Christian again. When I was in town back in Atlanta, I'd go to a church that I really liked. And when it worked out during those times that I was able to have the girls, I'd take them to Bible school and tell them all about church, over and over. Things were good there. Some good seeds were being planted, and I felt God's pleasure.

By now I was praying a lot, telling God that I believed I couldn't go back to Indiana because of all those skeletons. I prayed those things with an open heart, waiting and willing to listen to what God might say to me, perhaps through a stirring in my heart or something somebody might say to me. My biggest concern about going back home was whether I could stay sober despite whom I might run into or what drinking spots might "call out" to me if I went anywhere near them. I just told God I couldn't go back there: I had a great job in Atlanta and doubted I could make a decent living being back in Indiana, at least in and around my hometown of Sullivan. The catch-22 was that the only way I could make a decent living doing what I knew meant lots of travel, but if I were taking care of my kids as part of primary custody, I wouldn't be able to travel. At least, that was my first thought. I kept praying about it for a couple of months. Finally, some kind of solution for me came when my mom told me that she and my dad would go get the girls every chance they'd get and would spend time with them. They were inspired to do this because they could see the girls getting worse all the time in their behavior and their attitude. They were growing up in a dysfunctional home that wasn't even really a home.

However, this didn't work out for the long term, either. I learned that one day when my mom called me crying.

"What's wrong?" I said.

"I just took the girls home and I can't go get them anymore. I can't handle it," Mom told me between sobs. "They're out of control. They're dirty. They're dressed in rags. I take them places, and before you know it they're out of control. I'm sorry, I just can't go get them anymore."

Indiana Wants Me

At that point, I knew I had to go back to Indiana. I was going to have to give up my career, at least one version of it that promised upward mobility for me in a professional sense. Things were good and my life was good; I didn't want to give it up but I had to. I packed up everything and headed back to Indiana. God was telling me to return home and take care of my kids.

When I got back to Indiana, I stayed with my parents. Soon the girls started playing softball. They were seven and five years old, respectively, by now and were both on the team. I'd only been back for two weeks when I was approached by a woman I knew, telling me that she was dating the guy who previously had dated my ex-wife.

"There's bad things going on with your ex," this woman told me.

I didn't know this woman really well and couldn't recall ever having spoken to her before. I ended up keeping the girls from my ex and not returning them. The police called me about it and told me I just couldn't grab and take them away, that I had to file a complaint with them.

I had grown up with a guy who was now an attorney with Child Protective Services, so I paid a visit to him at his house and told him what was going on, relaying to him everything that woman had told me. He said I should file the complaints with the CPS. I called them and filed complaints on everything that was going on. In doing so, I also told them the name of the woman who had told me all about this stuff, giving them her name and contact info while also telling them that she had promised to testify on my behalf. I was soon told there would be an investigation.

My friend, the CPS attorney, called the CPS director on a Sunday to let her know what was going on and what needed to be done from a legal standpoint.

From that point on, I kept the kids and wouldn't take them back to my parents' house. Instead, we stayed in a hotel down the road where no one would be able to find us. I wanted to do this until any investigations were over with because, as I soon found out, Child Protection Services is just as corrupt as anyone else. I thought I was doing right thing. But my ex-wife was told what I was doing (but not where). She called me and started accusing me of taking them out of state.

I told her, "I live in Indiana."

"Well, you're taking them to Georgia."

"I don't live in Georgia anymore," I said. "I live in Indiana," and I left it at that.

CPS never did investigate. They never called the woman who had tipped me off to get testimony from her. This went on for about two and a half weeks before they filed for an emergency hearing, claiming I had kidnapped the kids. I was harassed by the police. The school harassed me. I kept the kids hidden. CPS never would investigate. When the case went to court, I was found in contempt of court. The woman who was director of CPS testified against me, saying stuff that wasn't even true, just making things up, like falsely claiming that I was going to run out of state with the girls.

I was ruled in contempt because I had kept the girls away from my ex for that time I had sequestered ourselves in an out-of-town hotel. So she got the girls back. As far as I know, CPS never did investigate—for one thing, they never interviewed me before the case went to court. On top of all that, I had to pay my ex's attorney's fees. A friend of mine had run into her attorney at a local tavern, where the attorney, my friend said, was joking and laughing, saying something to the effect of, "I'll take his money all day 'cause there's no way possible he'll have his girls."

I went back to work, and nothing changed on behalf of my daughters. My parents bought another house, and I ended up living in that house. I was still able to keep the girls with me a lot, while I was working for my brother, Tony, and traveling a lot. When I pulled back into town after completing a job somewhere, I would pick up the girls and they would stay with me until I left town. If I was in town, they were with me 100 percent of the time. I got free rein as far as custody, and my ex didn't object because to her I was a free babysitter.

This is the lifestyle I settled into for several years. My ex had primary custody, but I was spending more time with them than she was, and she didn't care about that at all. I kept telling myself, *I'm not going to give up*, but that vow sure came with some tests for me.

Stuff like that went on a lot. When I would return home and have them over to my house, I would ask them what they had been doing while I was gone. On many occasions, they would both break down crying, saying they couldn't tell me. What had happened, as I eventually found out, was that while I was two thousand or however many miles away, she'd be out drinking somewhere, probably getting drunk, while leaving them with somebody else, with whom I wasn't acquainted, to watch after them.

Several times I would call CPS and tell them what was going on. But that was useless; they *still* wouldn't investigate. I believe it was all a set-up. Other people would call CPS about the problem, and it still wouldn't do any good—they wouldn't check it out or go out and interview anyone. Here my kids are being neglected and there was nothing I could do. I've never felt so helpless, even during those times I was drunk. My parents and I would talk about it, and we couldn't figure out what we could do.

Finally, in 2007, I started keeping track of the days the girls were with me so I could document what was going on. At another hearing concerning a related issue, I spotted my ex-wife's attorney and my attorney walking down the sidewalk, patting each other on the back. I knew at that point that I had been had. My attorney was from a small, nearby town. It seems everyone knew everyone else. Then there was the time when I was notified of another upcoming hearing to be held on such and such day and time. I was in South Dakota on a job and had to leave, buy a plane ticket, fly back to Indiana, and rent a car. When I got there, someone had forgotten to let the judge know about the hearing, so it never happened. The judge was on vacation. So I lost the money from being on the job, plus the expense of everything.

I think everything combined related to this custody issue added up to close to a hundred thousand dollars over a five-year period. There were also times when I had the girls and was supposed to fly out on a job and meet the ex early in the a.m. to swap off the kids with her, and she wouldn't show, and I would miss my flight. That sort of thing happened numerous times, and still Child Protective Services didn't lift a finger; apparently, they didn't care. I'd have to buy another plane ticket, and that added up. It was killing me to live there.

I eventually took a job in Indianapolis about an hour and a half from Sullivan. They gave me a nice, big office, so that was good. After a while I decided to look for an attorney in Indianapolis who wouldn't in any way be connected to my small hometown and part of whatever game was going on there. I opened up the Indianapolis phonebook and quickly saw pages of what had to be a thousand attorneys listed. I immediately prayed, "Oh, God, help me find an attorney." I turned several pages, and an ad jumped out at me, grabbing my attention. It was an all-female firm specializing in family law. At first I thought it had to be a twist of fate. Here I was, a single dad, trying to get custody of two little girls, and you want me to hire an all-female law firm? But the more I thought about it, the better it sounded. I decided to go with it and see what would happen. By the time I dialed their number to call them, I was quite comfortable I was making a good decision.

I went and talked to the firm's associates and they said, "Yeah, we can win it for you, but it's going to cost you thirty to fifty thousand dollars when all is said and done." They told me they needed five thousand down to take the case. They also let me know I wasn't going to be able to live in Indy anymore. Even if I won the case and custody of the girls, I would not be able to change their residence; they would need to stay in whatever school they were enrolled in, and that meant staying in Sullivan.

Based on my experience in rural Indiana battling my ex-wife for custody, it seemed clear to me that custody laws still leaned heavily in favor of women, regardless of any one woman's character and poor lifestyle habits. I have since learned that such laws have gravitated to being more "open-minded," taking a closer look at both parties to see how fit either is in terms of parental care of the children involved. Per an article I found at divorcenet.com, "There was once a presumption that children should always stay with their mother following a divorce. Most states no longer honor that presumption, however. (In fact, some states have passed laws stating that there is no custody preference for women over men.)

"Despite this change, mothers are still more likely to get custody when parents divorce. State laws vary as to what courts must consider in determining custody arrangements, but the general standard used today is that the custody award must be in the 'best interests of the child.' And, the factors courts consider in discerning where those best interests lie are more likely to favor mothers, as most marriages are structured."[7]

My translation of that: even though the climb isn't as steep as it used to be, it's still an uphill battle for divorced men, even those who have proved themselves "A-rated" dads who have demonstrated skill in raising a child and keeping a hand in the process. Back home in Sullivan County, Indiana, however, at least a little over a decade ago, thanks to the intervention of Child Protective Services (or, actually, nonintervention in terms of my ex-wife) it was still a 1950s mentality when the calendar said it was the early 2000s.

Because I was so close to my parents and appreciated their counsel and continued support, I went and told them what was going on. I told them I had a law firm that could win the case for me—for us, actually—but that I didn't have the money to pay for it. By this time, I was already broken-hearted, figuring this might be the last step available to me, an expensive, last-ditch effort at that. I'd done all I could do. About a week later my dad called me and said come to their house, about a half-hour away.

When I got to my parents' house, we sat down at the dinner table.

"We want you to fight for your girls," they told me. "We'll help you financially. We've mortgaged the house. Here's the down payment, and we have the money to pay the rest of it, whatever you need. We just want you to do this." And with that, they handed me a check. It was an overwhelming moment for me: How many grandparents would do that for their grandkids? My parents had

---

[7] Lisa Guerin PhD, "Divorce for Men: Why Do Women Get Child Custody More Often?," divorcenet.com, date unknown, https://www.divorcenet.com/resources/divorce/for-men/divorce-for-men-why-women-get-child-custody-over-80-time, viewed June 8, 2021.

worked hard their whole lives. They had saved a little bit of money, and they had this big, beautiful house.

I went back to Indianapolis and paid the attorneys to start the process. As they had advised me earlier, I quit my job in Indy and moved back to Sullivan. By then I had made a huge file out of all that documentation I had been keeping. I had kept it on my computer and had also gotten a printer so I could be ready to produce it and hand it over to the lawyers when they asked for it. By now it was October 2007.

Let me backtrack here just a bit. Two months earlier, before hiring the Indy attorneys, I had told the girls' mother, "I'm tired of the girls living this way; I'm tired of your lifestyle." I even told her that while I had been living in Atlanta after taking that job with TerraCom, my main reasons for dreading a return to Sullivan was because of her and her lifestyle. I told her, "If you give up your lifestyle, I'll buy you a house and a car." I didn't want to give up my career, and so I begged her to take my offer, and she still wouldn't do it. I said, "You've got one year to get your life together. If you don't have your life together a year from now, I will take custody of these kids." She just laughed because she had been told so many times by her attorney that there was no way I would ever get custody, and she believed it.

About two years earlier, I also consulted with a friend of mine who was a local judge. He said, "Come on over to my house, and we'll talk a little bit." I went over and sat at his kitchen table and asked him if he thought I could get custody. He said, "Mike, I see no way possible that you could ever get custody of your girls." A friend of mine who is a prosecutor told me the same thing. I'm thinking they just don't know my God and what my God can do.

It was after all this, my last-gasp attempt to get this settled on my own, that I hired the Indy all-female firm. They quickly filed for a custody evaluation. It would be a "he said/she said" deal. Nobody on my ex-wife's side wanted to let the girls talk. I wanted them to talk because I knew they could win it for me—and that the truth needed to get out despite all the local resistance to it. She didn't want to let the kids talk because she knew they would tell everything she didn't want out in the open. We filed a custody evaluation, went to court for that, and the judge agreed to a custody evaluation.

The court put together a list of three evaluators, each of whom was qualified to handle a case like this. My wife's side in the case would be allowed to remove one person from the list, and my side could remove one of the others, and the one left would be the court-appointed evaluator. This was done in the name of fairness and objectivity, something that had been lacking in my case for years thanks to the inside job the "professionals" in my hometown had pulled on me. One thing I now had going for me was a staff of attorneys much better and much smarter than the Podunk attorney/boyfriend my ex had on her side.

We ended up with an evaluator who was not only a psychologist, a PhD, but also an attorney with a great reputation in the court system, someone who wasn't going to let local gamesmanship roll over anybody as it had done to me. The evaluation was eventually set up for April 2008. At the same time this was going on, I had started going to the First Christian Church of Sullivan. It was a really good church. They had a terrific children's program and offered a day camp that my girls went to and established a solid connection there.

I'd been raised in the Catholic church, so this was all new to me, but I needed to be prepared for what I hoped would come next. I figured if I won primary custody of the girls, I would need exactly the kind of support that I came to know this church would offer. I attended First Christian throughout the winter. By April they had a tent revival going on, right around the time the custody evaluation was to take place. At different times I thought about going forward and giving my life to Christ, something I obviously hadn't done yet but needed to do. I was overdue. As a Catholic, I had been baptized at birth, but had never really committed my life to Christ. It's a personal decision and, as a baby, you obviously can't make that decision.

I was at the tent revival the day before the evaluation was to take place, two hours away from Sullivan, and I would need to go and stay in a hotel there. At the tent revival that night, I went forward and gave my life to Christ. I felt like I was floating on air that night as I drove the two hours to the hotel. I knew things were going to go okay, that this evaluation was going to go well. The girls went over there with their mom and they, too, stayed in a hotel.

The next day's evaluation was a fairly long process, and lasted much of the day. The evaluator evaluated my ex and me together at the same time, and then each of us separately. He evaluated her with the girls, me with the girls, and the girls by themselves. We both then took a questionnaire with six hundred-plus questions. It was a very in-depth evaluation, and I felt good about it.

I was at peace during the entire evaluation. I was where I needed to be, on top of my game in terms of presenting myself and making my case with clarity, humility, and confidence. I've sat in enough business meetings over the years to know the importance of "being in the moment" as they say, and speaking clearly and concisely, from my heart as well as my head, while showing a good grasp of the history and details that had been going on; in short, I was pretty comfortable the whole time. Nothing asked of me surprised me, worried me, or put me on the defensive—I had nothing to be defensive about. I had been sober for five years now and had done nothing unworthy of a dad. I told everything about myself and left no openings that would allow the ex to badmouth me. I spoke with honesty about my past and what I had done.

Now the waiting game began.

A month later we got the evaluator's report, advising us that there would be a change of custody to the father—me. It had come out in my favor. I had fully expected that to happen; nonetheless, I was overjoyed. By now it was May 2008.

I was still not out of the woods, however. Once again, there were other issues dealing with Child Protection Services, such as when I was certain that CPS had enough cause to take my two daughters away from Joanna and return them to me. But CPS never did anything about it, essentially just turning their backs. Joanna would return home at night, apparently intoxicated, and pass out on multiple occasions. My daughters weren't able to wake her until morning. They would often cry themselves to sleep.

When I found out about this, I notified CPS, but they didn't do anything except tell me they were old enough to take care of themselves—at age nine and seven, respectively. When I then told the court-appointed evaluator about these two instances, his first question to me, a rhetorical one I presume, was why CPS had done nothing about this.

I told him this was old news with CPS, that they never had done a lick of investigating this case. He looked at me and said, "You know, if I say we need an emergency hearing, that's the icing on the cake and you'll have these girls." He said, "I want you to look at me right now and promise me that you will give your all to always take care of these girls and to raise them right." I looked right back at him and said, "You have my word." He signed off on it and sent a letter to the court saying we needed an emergency hearing.

The emergency hearing was held in July, and the evaluator informed the court of everything he had been told, and it wasn't a pretty picture. My parents were there and I was on my game when he questioned me. The only way I could describe it is that I had the Holy Spirit in me, because I sounded better than any presidential candidate. I had my (stuff) together. When I had given my life to Christ and gotten rebaptized, my mother bought me a cross. I had it on the whole time I was in court, and kept praying silently to myself. I will concede one point of gratitude to my ex—a month earlier she had agreed to let the girls be baptized, so I got my girls baptized. They had wanted to be baptized. Just a month before that, she had said she didn't want them to be baptized. It wasn't the sort of thing she was into. I wanted to know that they're baptized and saved even if I lost this thing and moved away. In June they got baptized, and my parents attended. A couple of weeks before that, I had gotten rebaptized, this time as an adult.

I heard the judge say, "I hereby grant emergency custody to be given to the father immediately." Then he started in on my ex. He looked at her and said, "You just don't get it, do you?" He lectured her for ten minutes about everything that had been going on because the girls had finally had a chance to tell their story. That's all they wanted—to be heard. Some parents don't want their children to be heard like that; they'd rather hide the truth.

My mom and dad were sitting there and they were smiling. At one point the judge asked, "Why wasn't CPS called?" He was then told CPS had been notified numerous times and had refused to investigate. He said, "Oh, Sullivan County," which apparently had a reputation beyond its borders for this sort of thing. Here's even the judge wondering aloud why CPS wasn't doing anything about what was going on with my ex and our daughters, then acknowledging that it wasn't a shock considering this had been taking place in Sullivan County. In recent years, the Sullivan County CPS has been restaffed by competent and honest people, and I believe they do a fair and honest service to the children of Sullivan County.

Obviously, my wife was kind of in shock after the judge made his ruling to give me custody. I went out to my truck, and she called me almost immediately, saying, "When do you want to start this?" and I said, "Right now. I'll pick them up." They were at a day camp at the church. I explained to them after I picked them up that they were going to be living with me, and they were pretty excited. With this latest ruling, the ex still had visitations—a couple of nights during the week plus every other weekend.

The emergency hearing had been in July. Then, in the middle of August, my dad and I took my daughters down to Gulf Shores, Alabama, for a mini-vacation before school started. Then came another wave of problems. My ex was at it again. We came back and they started school that week. They had been in school only two days when I learned their mom had called CPS, saying that in taking the girls to Alabama, my dad and I had pretty much just fed them KitKats and potato chips, and that they had been stung by jellyfish and we hadn't gotten any medical treatment for them. She also claimed that I was locking them in the house and that I had no food in my house.

It was all crazy. This time, however, CPS investigated immediately. *Now*, suddenly, they wanted to know what was going on. They had long ignored me when I tried to file complaints, but now that my ex was the one filing the complaint—a bogus one at that—they perked up and went right to work, as if answering a fire alarm! Apparently the emergency hearing judge's ten-minute lecture to my ex about all the stuff she had done in recent years hadn't resonated with the folks at CPS. In fact, they had already been to the school and questioned the girls without my knowing about it.

I got home just in time to greet the girls getting off the school bus, with them running up to me and telling me what was going on. I was like, "Are you kidding? How can this be?" To say I was upset doesn't come close to covering it. I found a note on the front door of my house from a CPS caseworker saying she needed to talk to me immediately. I broke down right there on the front porch in front of the kids. It was the first time they had ever seen me cry. *Why won't they leave us alone? Why can't we get on with our lives? When are these clowns ever going to take an ounce of initiative to investigate my ex?* The girls were upset, too. They insisted they had told the caseworker that they were fine and there had been no problem during the trip to the Gulf Shores.

I knew this caseworker who had interviewed my girls and left the note at my house. She had been working at the courthouse in the prosecutor's office and a couple of weeks earlier had started as a caseworker with CPS. She had been aware of the situation with the girls before this. When I spoke with her, I told her about all the times that CPS had been called about my ex's behavior and negligence, and nothing had been done by CPS then. Not ever.

She came out to my house, and I showed her all the food in the refrigerator. She said, "I don't need to investigate. I've already been to the school. I asked the girls if they were okay and they said, yeah, they were fine. They said as long as they're with their dad, they're fine." It was good for me to hear this, but I was still upset over the way that CPS had been conducting its business, being so one-sided and out of touch. I did get on her case a bit, sternly saying, "You already knew about all these calls and complaints that had been made to CPS, and they never investigated, until now. . . . I get custody and a month later they show up on my door." I was ticked, and she needed to know why I was rightfully ticked, because she was now a part of their team.

Let me take a brief break here to point out something I haven't touched on yet, but which needs to be brought out. By now, all this stuff between Joanna and me, with the divorce and now the custody battle, had been ongoing for about five years. Courtney and Grace were constantly caught in the middle of this—not just the irresponsible, neglectful behavior of their mom—but also the fact that their parents were battling each other, sometimes in front of them. By now they were nine and seven, respectively, and I had put them in counseling for some of this time. Courtney, now twenty-three and married, explains:

"My dad had us go to counseling a number of different times. I was like seven or eight at the time, and Grace five or six. We went to three or four different counselors. I remember having really bad anger problems growing up that I had to go to counseling for, which probably was from all of the trauma growing up that I don't really remember. Other than that, I don't really recall having counseling specifically (related to) their divorce.

"One thing that really stuck with me is what the last counselor I went to said to me: 'Any time that you're feeling overwhelmed or super stressed, the best thing to do is just isolate yourself from everyone and just kind of let yourself cool down. Get away from everyone, and then go back to just being your regular self.' I still do that, and it helps."

After all this with CPS's going to interview my girls at school, etc., there was still one more level of court hearing to go—what was called a final hearing. It was to be in November 2008, a hearing to actually determine final custody, once and for all. I guess that's sort of like in the movie *Animal House*, where the college dean tells the misbehaving frat boys he is putting them on probation, only for them to remind him they are already on probation, to which he testily replies, "Well, now you are on double-secret probation."

What I already had was actually described as "temporary emergency custody." I still didn't have full custody, and my ex knew that, meaning she wasn't finished trying to foil my getting custody of the girls. That door was still cracked open for her, and she kept her foot right there.

She was now working as a waitress at a restaurant. I knew another woman who also worked there and she told me, "You know about her going to the hospital, right?" I said no. She said, "Yeah, she overdosed on some drugs; she was trying to kill herself or something." Well, I'm now thinking this is what I need to go into this hearing with. So I called my attorneys and they subpoenaed the medical records from the hospital. We got to court and a woman arrived from the hospital with my ex's medical records. The doctor who did the original evaluation of my ex was also there, as were her attorney and my attorney. Her family was there, as was mine. Yes, it was a big deal.

My ex's side knew they were beat. For one thing, she was still drinking. (I had quit five years earlier.) They settled with my attorney before it got to the judge. They knew if this went to the judge, they would probably not only lose full custody, but overnight visitations as well. We then went before the judge and said, "Here's our agreement, and we both swore to it." My ex would not get overnight visitation until she went to and completed intensive rehab, which, as far as I know, she never did. I had full custody at this point. She had no overnights. I now had them 365 days and nights a year. They also ordered that she had to abstain from drinking for twenty-four hours prior to having the kids at all; nor could she drink at any time the kids were in her custody. I'm pretty sure she violated that no-drinking rule a lot. My kids would take pictures of the cups she used for drinking and said they smelled like alcohol.

A month after I got full custody, my ex married a guy sixteen years older than her, and she's still married to him to this day. About six months after she remarried, she went to some little recovery group and sent notice to the court about that, claiming that

that fulfilled her rehab obligation and that this should qualify her to get overnights with the girls. It got shot down by the court. That recovery group is not rehab, and chances are she was still drinking. No matter, both girls are adults now and they can make their own choices in terms of visiting their parents. By the way, my ex now lives close to Santa Claus, Indiana, while every day for me is now like Christmas, for I have been sober for eighteen years, born again through Jesus Christ for thirteen years, and in a close, loving, secure relationship with both of my grown, beautiful daughters.

Those are among the rewards for having been Mr. Mom for a number of years, a fulltime position from 2008 on. It was a role I felt prepared for and certainly one that I relished, now that I had full custody. But a few more bumps in the road awaited during those Mr. Mom years, as you will see in the next chapter.

Before I bring this chapter to close, I offer a few tips for well-meaning, divorced dads trying to navigate a custody process still tilted in favor of women. Some of these are my own tips; others are sourced from elsewhere:

1. Play by the rules and the laws, no matter how exasperating they can be. Breaking the law in a desperate attempt to win primary custody will bite you big in the long run, perhaps sooner. It's not worth it.
2. Be persistent and resilient in your pursuit of a righteous victory in your favor. Be prepared for a virtual punch or two to your gut along the way, when things don't go your way. It's going to be a fight, and I don't mean become a pugilist. Be emotionally ready for those times, but remain steadfast in your heart and stay cool in your head. Stay the course; stay strong.
3. Keep the faith. If you are a Christian, if you have a personal relationship with God and faith in Jesus Christ, pray

for guidance and at least *expect* favor every step of the way. If you aren't a Christian, seek Him out and be willing to take the walk to the altar. God has your back; he's always had mine, even when I had departed from him.

4. Document everything; keep records of issues you spot concerning your partner's treatment of and relationship to the children—i.e., problem areas.[8] Keep detailed dates, times, and descriptions, beginning as soon as you suspect your marriage may be headed to the rocks, and beyond. Such documentation can serve you well once CPS, attorneys, law enforcement, etc. get involved.
5. Choose an experienced, skilled family law attorney. Seek credible referrals. Don't just open the Yellow Pages with your eyes closed and pick out whomever your finger goes to. Even if they charge more per hour than you had anticipated, those extra dollars spent could save you a whole lot of headaches and heartache on the back end.
6. Don't use the children as pawns. Big no-no. You want them to come through this as unscathed as possible, but there will likely be ramifications anyway; counseling might be necessary at times. When you are and your spouse or ex-spouse are in the presence of any or all of your children, keep your cool to the highest degree and don't berate or vilify your spouse in front of them.[9]
7. Don't trust anyone except your attorney(s), and even then

---

[8] Brad Micklin, "5 Custody Tips for Dads Who Want Full Custody of Their Kids, divorcemag.com, March 27, 2019, https://www.divorcemag.com/articles/custody-tips-for-dads, viewed June 9, 2021.

[9] Chase Scheinbaum, "8 Tips for Dads in Child Custody Battles, According to Fathers Who've Been There," fatherly.com, March 29, 2021, https://www.fatherly.com/love-money/10-tips-for-surviving-custody-battles-experienced-fathers/, viewed June 9, 2021.

maybe not even him or her. Think like a lawyer, as fatherly.com suggests, adding, "Understand that any text messages, emails, or social media posts can be discoverable and be entered in court. Be careful and cognizant of who you write to, and what about."[10]

[10] Chase Scheinbaum, "8 Tips for Dads in Child Custody Battles, According to Fathers Who've Been There,"

8

Mr. Mom and Beyond

I WISH DEALING WITH LIFE'S DIFFICULTIES was as easy as removing that annoying pebble from your shoe, but, as we all know, life isn't always fair. Some people are just born or raised to be that pesky pebble that sneaks its way into someone else's shoe and won't go away.

Although I got a favorable ruling in that 2008 hearing to determine final custody of the two girls, my ex remained a thorn in my side even though I rarely saw her or spoke to her. But my story is incomplete without my telling what happened in 2012, when the other shoe dropped again. This was a full four years after the final custody decree and well into my enjoying my new life and teaching myself how to raise my daughters, complete with the usual parenting ebbs and flows. By this time I had become pretty secure in my belief that I was finally home-free from all that divorce and custody battle stuff. If nothing else, what I'm about to recall offers a testimony of how devoted and determined I was to putting parenthood ahead of every other thing going on in my life.

It was in July or August 2012 that my younger brother, Tony, called me to tell me he had a friend in Miami who needed a construction manager and wanted to know if I'd be interested in taking the job. This was exactly the kind of thing I needed. For several years as a full-time dad, I had been doing whatever I could for work. That entailed stretching dollar after dollar to make ends meet, as my new parenting commitment meant I had to stay home more. That meant not being able to fill as many contracts as I would have liked.

When Tony called and explained to me what was going on and what the job in Miami involved, I said, "Heck, yeah, I'd love to pack the girls up and move to Florida." They were no longer spending a whole lot of time with their mom at that point. So I called the company myself to set things up with them, and they said they needed me to be available to start in a couple of weeks. I called my attorneys to see if this would be okay, for me to pack up the girls and move them with me to Florida. They said, "Yeah, you'll be able to do that." They told me the state law in Indiana says you have to give ninety days' notice to the ex-spouse in order to relocate any dependent kids like this, but that shouldn't be a problem considering the situation I was in. I now had full-time primary custody, plus my ex by now was barely having any contact with the girls anyway.

I again called the company in Miami and told them I would accept their offer. That was exciting. It was a high-paying job, a white collar job. I would have been set. No more financial woes, no more having to live like a hermit much of the time. My career really would be in good shape after years of struggle and anxiety. We were renting an old house, and everything we had in the house was hand-me-down furniture somebody else had given us.

You can guess what happened next—the best-laid plans of mice and men. My ex-wife filed an objection to my moving the girls out of state with me, and a hearing date was scheduled. I again asked my attorneys if they were certain that there would be no problem with all this, and they assured me that I would prevail and be able to accept the job and take the girls to Florida with me on a permanent basis, not just one of those seven-week temporary stays. Once I got that assurance, I was able to call my bosses-to-be in Florida, explain my situation, and get an additional two weeks to get down there—figuring I wouldn't even need all of that time, but let's just play it safe, just in case.

Confident of my imminent move with the girls in tow, I took care of everything before making such a big move. I told my landlord I was moving out and then got rid of nearly everything we owned, either throwing it out or giving it away. Plus, my mom had agreed to go to Florida with us to help take care of the girls while I was working. By now Courtney was fourteen and Grace twelve, and they were pumped about moving to Florida with the warmer climes, plenty of sand and water, and the chance to meet more cute beach boys in a day than they had seen in their young lives up to that point (not that that enthused their protective dad a whole lot). Everything was soon gone. The washer and dryer. Every piece of furniture. No beds to sleep on. I was going to rent what we needed once we got to Florida with an eye to buying a house of our own with our own furniture in the not-too-distant future. Soon I would be able to afford all that.

In my mind, we were already halfway to Florida.

We went into the hearing and it didn't take long for the judge to land his first punch to my gut. He said, "You've got to give ninety days' notice, and I'm going to hold you to that." Not only that, it was also the ex's weekend for visitation, which compounded what I was feeling. I was horribly devastated, to put it mildly. We had lost everything we owned, giving it away, and I lost the job. Now we were essentially stranded, and we hadn't budged a mile.

After leaving the courthouse, I went straight home to tell the girls and my mom, who was babysitting them while I was at the hearing. Sadness all around. So the girls went with their mom to spend the evening. That was the most excruciatingly difficult part about those twenty-four hours. Not only had I lost a chance to make new beginnings for my daughters and me in the Sunshine State, but my ex also got to stick my nose into the stink once again by taking them home with her—although who's to say how much time, if any, she spent being a mom to them once she got them to her house.

My only option was to stay home by myself. That meant sleeping on the floor because I no longer had a bed. My brother, Tony, found out what was going on and got ticked because this was a friend of his from the past. My mother told me I should just go ahead and go to Florida myself. The judge had said to just leave them with their mom until the ninety days are up, then I could come back and get them. Still, I kept thinking I had worked so hard to get these girls. Plus, my ex and her attorney were in cahoots together, and I know they were sleeping together for a while. This wasn't going to be easy.

Later that night I told my brother that I was going to go ahead and go. So that night I called Courtney, now fourteen, and told her, "Dad is going to go ahead and go. I'm going to leave you with your mom and come back and get you later." But I could just hear it in her voice—the disappointment and fear; she and Grace were in a bad situation. I didn't sleep a wink that night. I said to myself, *This is bull. We'll starve to death, but I am not letting her have those kids. If I let her have those kids, she and her attorney will work out some kind of deal and then drag it out in court five more years, then I'm screwed.*

The next morning, bright and early, I called Courtney and told her, "Daddy is not leaving you. Daddy is coming to get you.

We're staying together. We ain't got nothing. We'll start over, but we're staying together, the three of us." She was happy to hear that. My mom, however, was mad at me for not taking the job. Tony was so angry because I wouldn't leave my kids that he wouldn't speak to me for three months. Luckily, the landlord hadn't rented our house yet, so we kept our house and were able to pick up some furniture here and there.

That weekend, while Courtney was back staying with her mom, she was playing on her mom's phone when she found a text between her mom and her attorney, mentioning something about how I would be making a hundred fifty thousand dollars a year at that job in Miami. The text from her attorney said, "We win, and with that hundred fifty thousand dollars a year, you'll have full custody and you'll never have to work again." The ex and her attorney had planned it out all along. If I had given her the girls, I would have never gotten them back. The girls would have been stuck in that same lousy situation again, right back where they were. I was pretty devastated, and on top of that I didn't have any work.

The girls are close, and I'm close to my daughters—I talk to them every day. Joanna hadn't had overnight visitation with them for three years, but I finally gave up and let her have overnight visitation again. When the girls were about fifteen and thirteen, she was forcing them to come see her. She would say, "It's my visitation and I'm going to take it." I finally sat down one day and wrote her a letter telling her that forcing the girls to spend overnights with her was not doing any good. "They were already counting the days until they didn't have to come and see you again." For some strange reason, she asked the girls, "Is that letter your dad wrote how you really feel?" They were like, yeah, and at that point she quit forcing the overnight visitations on them. And they quit going as soon as she quit forcing them. For about the last seven or eight years now, they have not been to see her with any regularity. It's been tough, but I'd do again what I did then in a heartbeat—staying put in Indiana and not taking the job in Miami.

Trials, Tribulations, and Triumphs for a Mr. Mom

As happy as I was back in 2008 when I finally got full custody of Courtney and Grace, I was also confronted by the stark reality of being a Mr. Mom. If you ever want to see a good movie that depicts the life of a dad acting as the primary caregiver of young children, at least during the day, you should see *Mr. Mom,* a funny yet revealing movie starring Michael Keaton as a stay-at-home dad who has just been laid off at work. He's staying home with the young kids while his wife goes back to her well-paying but long-hours position in corporate marketing so they can continue to pay their bills and live comfortably. It's a comedy, as you might have guessed, and Keaton is terrific as the dad who discovers a side of life—an icky one at times—that he had never really seen or experienced before. I'm no Michael Keaton, of course, who strikes a great balance of anxiety, panic, and humor in playing the role, but a good portion of the movie rings true when it comes to being a Mr. Mom in real life. Such as handling a small child's problems related to certain bodily functions on how the dad is treated in public, often with scorn, by other women who resent the fact that he is a married man out of work and fulfilling a role usually handled by the wife, at least in the early 1980s.

What made it especially tough for me in those early years of raising our daughters essentially on my own was my work situation. The job in Miami could have solved a lot of ills, but it didn't work out, and that's by my choice. It was all I could do to scratch out a fairly meager living, but we managed—the girls and I.

"There's just been a lot of things he's had to rebuild, you know, for himself—I mean he had to grow up," my younger daughter

Grace, now twenty-one, said in an interview for this book. For the sake of honesty and objectivity, she was interviewed by someone other than me. "He had to grow up in a different way with a whole new perspective and with a sober mind, which is a big step for people, especially after living the way he did for so long." As I'm inserting her thoughts and insights into the book, I am reading these quotes—including Courtney's elsewhere in this book—for the first time. It's sobering to hear this, but I'm listening.

"Dad had to relearn, one, how to be human and, two, how to get back on his feet as an adult and not be excused for all of his behaviors," Grace said. "Plus, he has had to rebuild everything and get back on his feet at the same time he was raising us. He's just had to keep going because there was no going back. I don't think that was ever an option in his mind.

"Oh, we had to grow up, too. We had to grow up before, I guess, we were supposed to. My sister played a big part in being a parent to me. Me and her—we were parents to each other because our parents were still learning to be parents. I've been alongside my father through all of it, seeing different things and paying attention to the way he's helped people as well as seeing his own positive outcomes. You know, there's a lot there, but it's all understood. I mean, God has had a plan for him and that's that."

My older daughter, Courtney, now twenty-three and married, says she's blocked out those days with her mom, who really hasn't been a part of her life for several years now. The girls see her once every year or two and maybe talk to her every few months; I'm not really sure.

When I first took custody of the girls, they went through counseling for a while—it was part of a court order, although I would have taken them myself anyway, considering all they had been through and privy to. I think it really helped both of them, and I am very close to both of them. We talk a lot about a lot of things. They just kind of accept things as they are.

"I was always aware of the fact that we had it different in our household from most other kids, with our dad having full custody," Courtney said. "I've heard it said that if you have past childhood trauma, you mature a lot faster. And so I was always more aware of the situation and the fact that it was different, and that's why it didn't take that big a toll on me.

"Living with just my dad (with him now a single parent) was a whole different thing. Dads don't really have a whole lot of structure like moms do. My mom has had her issues, but we always had breakfast every morning and dinner every night. Plus, we had to do our homework by a certain time before we could go out and play. With my dad, we had dinner every night, but it wasn't always him making it. He could make things like spaghetti and pancakes, and that was about it.

"There were times on a school night we would be out in the front yard playing on the waterslide at like ten o'clock, which you wouldn't be doing at your mom's house because moms are usually more strict. Usually, that is. It was definitely a lot different for us. My dad was always like the fun dad because we got to do whatever we wanted, which was different from what a lot of other parents were doing in making their kids abide by a lot more (rules)."

The fact that I was raising two girls instead of, say, two boys, presented another set of challenges for me. Such as what to do when your little girls grow up and hit puberty, and suddenly feminine products come to the forefront, and Dad hasn't got a clue. I'll again let Courtney offer her take on things:

"Let's see, I was eleven when I started puberty, and we were living with my dad at the time," Courtney said. "I would text my mom to text my dad to tell him we needed to go get feminine products at the store, because I was so embarrassed to tell him this myself. So we go to the nearest convenience store/gas station and he'd be like, 'Okay, here's my (credit) card, go get what you need.' I'm like, 'I don't know what to get, I'm eleven.' As time went on, though, we got more comfortable with that sort of thing. By the time we got to middle school and high school years, we'd be in Walmart and he'd be like, 'Hey, you need any tampons or pads?' And I'm like, 'No, I'm good.' It became a more open subject between us, just as it was with boy problems. Having a sister helps with stuff like that, though, when we could bounce stuff off each other or with friends that we could trust going to with issues."

Financial Struggles

As I write this, in 2021, I've been sober for eighteen years dating back to 2003, five years before I got custody of the girls. Like I said, we struggled a lot financially. Case in point: my Ford truck had more than a couple of hundred thousand miles on it and was wearing out. I wanted to get something more practical for me and the kids now that I was raising them full time, but I also knew my credit wasn't very good. Seeking help or at least guidance, I went to see a guy I knew, and he went with me to look for a van. We found a really nice one we both liked, priced within range of what I thought (hoped) I could afford. He said he had a friend who worked for a finance company and that he would talk to her on my behalf to see if I could get financing to pay for the van. He called her and as a return favor to him for referring me to her—finance folks don't always approve loans, but they are always on the lookout for prospective customers—she agreed to approve me for a loan. We kept it for a couple of years, even though I was struggling to make payments on it. I was so broke, and we had all these bills.

I believed that with God's help, I could still make this happen. In that spirit, I wrote on a white board we had in the house a quote from the Book of Matthew that says, "With God all things are possible." We were going to survive, and I wanted to share that message with my daughters. I felt good about having God in my life as I went to bed that night, only to wake up the next morning to find out that the van had been repossessed. But I still had my old Ford truck, and we survived. I also went through four back surgeries in a stretch of seven years—chalk that up to the rigors of all the climbing I had done, and still was doing on occasion.

Making a Move

One thing I had done a year or two after getting full custody of the girls was moving with the girls to another town about thirty miles away. This was when the girls were about twelve and ten, and I did this to put a little more distance between us and my ex-wife so we could get farther away from her connections as well as some problems with the school and CPS bothering us for no reason. We just wanted a fresh start. My ex tried to fight us on that, but she had also moved about thirty miles away in the other direction, so I don't know what she was objecting to. What was done was done—we had moved. If we could've moved a thousand miles away, I would've done that.

Even after the move, the ex would stir up trouble for me, like the time Courtney, who was in the seventh grade at the time, let a friend of hers borrow her phone and forgot to get it back from her before the friend boarded her bus at the end of the school day to go home. Courtney was still waiting for her bus when she called me from the school, all stressed out and nervous because her friend now had her phone and lived on the other side of town. She said, "Dad, I messed up, and now I don't have my phone."

I'm like, "Okay. That's fine. No big deal." I mean, kids are kids, you know. "We'll just go get it after you get home."

Well, she gets off the school bus at home, and I'm cleaning

out the garage. As she walks up, I'm standing there with a shotgun that had been my grandpa's from something like a hundred years earlier and which had been handed down through the generations.

As she walks up, she starts laughing and says, "Am I in that much trouble?" And I said, "No. No. Of course not," and told her what I was doing. Well, she told her mom about it only because she thought it was funny. Next thing I know, her mom's attorney had filed papers with the court saying I was threatening my thirteen-year-old daughter with a shotgun. This is how asinine the stuff was I had to deal with.

At times, even the challenges of being a single dad paled in comparison to what I was having to deal with in the aftermath of a bad divorce that bookended a bad marriage. Many people don't accept single dads. I don't mean to be bitter about it, but it's a single mom's world out there when it comes to single parents. Mr. Mom doesn't have a prayer, at least not eight to twelve years ago when I was in the thick of it. Whenever you hear about charities for single parents, it's always "single mom" this and "single mom" that. Guys like me are lepers in that world. As a single dad with two young girls in school, I would sometimes have to go to the school for one reason or another; once I got there, the school admin assistants wouldn't want to talk to me, or if they did it would be with a chill in the air. Rudeness, 360 degrees. When I would visit the pediatrician with my two daughters, I'd be the only man in the whole place. Trust me when I say it was not smiles all around in the waiting room.

"Yeah, we dealt with a lot," Grace said. "Like ladies at the doctor's offices or at schools. It was tough because they weren't very respectful to him and toward us. They thought it was weird, or they just didn't look at a man the same as they would have with a mother or woman having the kids.

"There were a lot of disadvantages to that because, you know, he had to bite his tongue. And even with people at our church, women at our church, they were the same way to us. There are some that would love to help him out and give him pointers and help us girls. Then there were others who just couldn't believe that he was doing it. Instead of encouraging him, they discouraged him, and it wasn't always pleasant."

Even the radio deejays seemed to have it in for me, or at least Mr. Moms in general. There's a Christian rock station not too far away that I listen to quite a bit. Every year they would sponsor a "Single Mom Saturday," when they would give all these moms at different places a free car wash and a free oil change. I thought that was great. I had no problem with it. So I thought, *You know, that would be something good for single dads, too.* I decided to pursue it just to see how the station would respond. I sent emails to their two morning on-air personalities—one was female, the other male. I wrote, "You know, it would be great if you wouldn't discriminate against single dads. Just have a Single Parent Saturday to include dads as well as moms. Otherwise, it's discrimination." I was nice about it, noting that it was a Christian station, and "God bless you for what you're doing," and all that sort of thing.

Well, the woman deejay never responded to me, but the guy did, writing back, "Well, we rely on other charities to take care of single dads." So I emailed him back, "What charity would that be that helps out single dads?" And, of course, there isn't one; not around here anyway. He never followed up with a response. I kept thinking about that snub for two or three years, and even got to thinking about posting something on their Facebook page, telling them what I thought about them—nothing good—and that would be my way of revenge, making them look bad to their listeners, at least their male ones. But being a Christian, I remember

God saying in Scripture, "Revenge is mine." As Christians, we're not supposed to seek revenge, but rather to let God take care of the situation. So I let it go, finally.

Not long after that, the station's transmitter breaks, and guess who gets called to fix it? I go out there and fix their transmitter, and I got paid enough to cover my car washes and oil changes for the next twenty years. I did not price-gouge them. I just charged my standard rate for that kind of job, but I can tell you, it's not a cheap fix. God *did* take care of it for me. I should also point out that the broken transmitter was not right next to the station, so I wasn't in a position to knock on their door while at the job site so I could pursue a word with at least one of their deejays.

All things considered, it could be tough as a single dad with two little girls. Even at the church we were going to, there's always a mother-daughter overnight or father-son this or that, but the father-daughter thing just doesn't happen a lot. Once in a great, great while, there might be a father-daughter dance, but even at church a lot of people can't accept a single dad with two little girls.

Strong Girls

Courtney and Grace have always been a lot tougher than most kids their age. I hated it when they were having to go through what they did in having a front-row seat to what was happening when things really started falling apart between Joanna and me. But I look at them now, grown up and in their early twenties, and things have turned out pretty well for them, and they both have great futures. I believe that. They know about resilience and they both have developed thick skins without sacrificing such qualities as compassion and perseverance.

The three of us have been quite active in church, helping out with activities there and, of course, attending church and Sunday school. Our church had one of those deals where they had kids church going on at the same time the regular church service was taking place. Courtney would go to Sunday school and then to kids church, but most of the time Grace wouldn't go to kids church. She would want to stay in church with me. She didn't let me too far out of her sight. One time she was in trouble for something at home, and she knew I was upset and she said, "Dad, you need to be like Jesus and forgive." And I said, "Well, Grace, you're forgiven, but you're still in trouble." It's like with anybody who sins—Jesus will forgive you, but there are often still consequences of that sin you have to deal with.

Another thing we always did was pray before dinner. They both said the same prayer, always the exact same prayer. I would encourage them to do something different, but it was always the same one, which I finally accepted because at least they were praying before dinner. One thing I did with them from the time they were really young until they got up into their teens was, when it was bedtime, I would go into their bedroom and with my thumb make the sign of the cross on their foreheads and say a prayer over them. I did this, literally, thousands of times over the years. This way I always felt like they were blessed. My mother would sometimes do it to my brothers and me when we were young, and that's where I got the idea. When my girls went to bed, they knew to wait on me to come in there to give them their blessing.

There were other times they just wanted to do something to get out of the house. There was one time, probably around the time they were in middle school, they came into my room around midnight and said, "Dad, we can't sleep. Can we go to Walmart?" I'm like, "Sure." So there we were at Walmart at about one in the morning on a school night, just looking around, doing some shopping. Yeah, there were times that I wasn't the strictest dad in the world. Here's the thing, though; I made it a point while my daughters were growing up that anytime they asked me to spend time with them, I would never turn them down. That's still the case, even though they are both now in their early twenties. Just before Grace turned twenty-one, it was a Saturday night and I was getting ready to go out of town, and I had about a million things to do. That's when Grace called and said she wanted to come over and hang out with me. Everything else could wait, and I spent several hours with her. After she left, I ended up working until past midnight to get everything done I needed to get done. Everything else goes by the wayside when they want to spend time with me. If you're not doing that with your kids, it's never too late to start. At least, I hope it's not too late.

When they were younger, they spent a whole lot of time with me, except for a period of a few years in there early on when I was out of town on a job. We traveled a little bit when they were growing up. We went to Florida a few times, although we couldn't afford to go to a lot of places. There were also times I took them with me on jobs, where I taught them things they could do to help me, like putting together a tower before we put it up. We also spent a lot of time at parks and swimming. At one time or another we must've gone to every swimming pool within fifty miles of home during the summer. We were always going, doing something, and we never sat still very long. I'm not one to sit still, and they've always been kind of restless themselves. I wonder where they got that.

One of our favorite places to swim was at a little beach called Fowler Park. It's a little county park with a really small beach, but it was free. Until my parents sold their house, we'd go swimming there because they had an in-ground pool. They also had a pond, and it seemed like the girls spent more time in the pond than they did in the pool. They just liked the pond. Dad had a big dock they would jump off of, and eventually I bought them little inflatable Jet Skis that were battery-powered. They could go all over the pond in them, and they had a blast. They had a lot of fun. They really got their full use out of them, and they both still love to swim to this day.

We always found new ways to have fun, especially in the summertime. I remember one time buying a big watermelon and cutting it up. We were getting ready to eat it when Grace said, "Dad, can we go on the roof and eat this watermelon?" She was talking about the roof of the house. The roof didn't have a real steep pitch to it—in fact, it was almost flat. I'm like, "Hey, why not?" So I got the ladder out, carried the watermelon slices up there, and all three of us sat on the roof and ate watermelon that summer day. It was some of the best-tasting watermelon that any of us have ever eaten.

We lived out in a very rural area. A blacktop road ran from in front of our house. Standing in the middle of it we could see a mile in either direction. That's Indiana for you. Many times on a hot summer night, Grace and I would go out there and lay in the middle of the road and look up at the stars. By then the temp had cooled down enough to keep us from getting burned from the blacktop, yet it still held just enough heat to keep us from getting uncomfortable. Like I said, you could see cars coming from a mile away, so there was no problem getting out of the way of whatever traffic came along, and there wasn't that much of it out as far as we were from everything.

As you might have guessed, I am a staunch believer of God and country. And I, for one, know that the cross is what you kneel for and the flag and the national anthem are what you stand for, with your right hand placed over your heart. The girls and I had the church and faith part down well. I also made it a point to teach them about respecting and honoring our soldiers, retirees, and veterans. One time when they were in middle school, there was going to be a local race on Memorial Day to honor our soldiers, especially those who had died for their country. My dad, a Vietnam veteran, had died that March, so I decided I was going to run it. Here I was, having had those back surgeries and other physical issues, but I started training for it. There was going to be a 5K and a one-mile run. I decided I was going to train for the 5K, which I finished, and the girls each ran the one-mile run. I even finished without stopping or walking along the way. That was kind of neat.

Another thing we've done together, not a whole lot, is shoot guns. The girls like to shoot, and we occasionally shoot.

Both girls were involved in more traditional sports. They played softball at a young age, and, by middle school, Courtney was really good at basketball. She played on a travel team that went around the state, but by her freshman year of high school she was burned out on basketball and stopped playing. I went to about every one of their games over the years, but I was not a yeller at games, coaxing on my daughters or telling the refs what they could be doing better. I pretty much kept to myself sitting there watching the games.

"I was like ten or eleven when I played baseball, and that was fun playing with the guys," Courtney said. "After that I just stuck to travel softball and basketball mainly. I ended up quitting basketball right before high school because I think my dad wanted me to play a little too much. I would play summer ball, Boys and Girls Club, school ball, and travel ball, and it was an all-year-round-thing. It can just wear out a fifteen-year-old."

In addition to playing softball, Grace was into track and played some basketball. Her main thing was track; she was a good runner and went to the county championships one year in track. She ran the 400 meters and was on a relay team. Grace was always really interested in gymnastics, and it bothers me to this day that she wasn't able to get more involved in the sport at an earlier age. Both girls wanted to try gymnastics, but their mom refused to take them because she had her own agenda, even though I offered to pay for it. I couldn't take them because I was gone much of the time. Courtney eventually lost interest in gymnastics, but several times over the years after the girls came to live with me, Grace would give gymnastics a try, only to find that all the other girls her age at the club had been doing it since they were toddlers. Grace was a good athlete, but because she was so far behind the rest of the girls, it was embarrassing for her and she eventually gave up. It was sad because she really wanted it so badly.

Both girls also played some soccer when they were young. Courtney was really good, and she was asked to play on some travel teams and stuff like that, so she tried out and made the team. Even though I didn't know much about the game and actually found soccer sort of boring, I accepted it and supported her if she wanted to go play with the team. But when we went out to eat after the tryouts, she said to me, "Dad, I really don't want to play soccer." And I was pretty happy about it, to be honest.

Being the sporting type of guy I am, at least at some level, I really enjoyed watching my girls participating in, and succeeding at, various athletic activities. One generation to the next, there was some bonding going on there. Another area of bonding which we shared and connected on at some level was my work. I would sometimes take them with me on the road to jobs. It would mean missing some school at times, but this wasn't about irresponsibly ditching school and playing hooky for the sake of kicks. It was borne out of necessity, both in terms of parental supervision and some grunt work I needed for them to do to help me complete the jobs and fulfill my contracts. A lot of it was tough work, and I would have to instruct them on some technical things—nothing dangerous or beyond the scope of their ages—and both demonstrated ample toughness, resilience, and know-how. They both were able to pick up on things pretty quickly and helped me out quite a bit.

Because I couldn't travel far with the girls, I went around to all these local places that had communication needs—like radio stations, power companies, sheriff's departments, emergency management places, internet companies, anybody that had any communication stuff that had towers. I worked for universities, too. With all that, I was able to build up a pretty good clientele—anyone who had a tower within a fifty- or sixty-mile radius, I had their business.

I made good money doing it, but there wasn't enough of it. I'd be lucky if I'd get a call every two or three weeks to go do some tower work. Plus, I didn't have a crew—I didn't have enough of a steady volume of work to justify having one. All I had were me and my two young daughters; they were my crew.

I'd climb up by myself and then had everything in terms of equipment, devices, etc., prepared on the ground beforehand. I would extend the rope from up on my perch, so all they would have to do was hook it on for me and I'd pull it up.

My oldest daughter, Courtney, was twelve years old and I had her putting together tower sections on the ground. I have pictures of it somewhere. When Grace was fifteen she helped me install a piece of equipment two hundred and fifty feet in the air; she climbed right up there and helped me install it.

"What we did in learning how to do these tasks was more of a step-by-step thing, with him telling us how to do something and then hoping we were doing it right," Grace said.

My daughters were pretty tough, and to this day are really good workers. They should be; I worked them. Courtney still works with me, and Grace helps me once in a while. They did stuff twelve- or fourteen-year old girls shouldn't have been out there doing, but we did what had to be done. Courtney later worked at Kroger for a while and the manager there said she was a good worker. She said she told the manager, "This is nothing; my dad's been working me like a slave since I was two years old."

"Last year (in 2020)," Courtney said, "I worked with my dad on the road from about May until December. And it was pretty exhausting performing all that tower work and doing the warehouse running, like getting all the antennas that were six or eight feet long. That stuff is super heavy. There's times he'd be like, 'Let me get that,' and I would be just hauling it over my shoulder. Like, *I don't need no man to get this for me*. Stuff like that. There was also a lot of traveling. So, I'm definitely glad to be home now."

Both of my girls have good work ethics. My dad—their paternal grandfather—was a really hard worker. He passed away in 2012 from lung cancer; he smoked like a freight train through the years. He had time to say his goodbyes and get his affairs in order. It wasn't a negative situation, because he was saved. The priest came and gave him his last rites. When Dad passed, my mother asked me and my brothers if we wanted to speak at his funeral. I said, "Yeah, I do." So I got up there at the church, the same church in which my parents got married. We come from this huge extended family, so there were a lot of people there. I got up there and said, "Mother asked me if I wanted to speak today and I said, 'Heck, yeah, I've waited forty years to get the last word in. I finally got the last word in.'" Dad's in a better place. No regrets on my part. We spent a lot of time together and got along really well. If I would have been him, I would have knocked the crap out of me a whole lot more.

Both of my daughters have climbed at different times. I taught them right. Courtney doesn't climb anymore; she does administrative work instead. Grace would climb up there on a sunny day and sit on the platform and listen to her headphones. She thought it was relaxing. Actually, it is kind of peaceful when you get up in the air like that. You're above everything else.

"I was about eight when I started working for him," Grace said. "I remember doing different stuff on jobs and really getting into it."

"There were multiple times we had to be on a job site helping him because he wasn't supposed to be on it by himself in case of an emergency," Courtney said. "I remember one time—I think it was my eighth-grade year—when it snowed really bad and schools up here ended up having to close for a couple of weeks. It had snowed four or five inches, and Grace and I were out in the snow helping him put together a tower. I ended up getting infected pneumonia in my lungs from it, but I bounced back. There've been times where I probably shouldn't have been helping him. Yet I've always been known for being able to lift a lot more than a normal girl could, and he needed the help at the job sites.

"At times I would help him hang guy wires for a tower; sometimes we had to paint something. On other occasions I helped him put together a couple of towers with the impact gun. And that's what we were doing when there's like a couple of inches of snow on the ground because you can't put it all together, like, on the ground. And in my later high school years, he had his internet business, so we were always running around, testing different products, being on the ground while he was hooking stuff up. It was nothing major. Sure it was probably stuff that most people might think teenage girls shouldn't be doing, but it builds character. It exposes you to responsibility and teaches you how to be resourceful. . . . During all this time, I managed to get my high school GED when I was sixteen and went on to get my associate's degree from Vincennes University, so whatever school time we missed didn't seem to hold us back."

When the girls were younger, and this was in 2009, I hurt my back while working on the roof of a house for a single mother. I don't know if it was from throwing shingles up on the roof or what it was exactly, but the doctor told me I had a joint problem causing the pain. I had to have surgery in which they inserted plates because of a problem with my tailbone and pelvis. However, the two plates never properly fused—these things were just grinding the whole time, and for several years I was absolutely miserable. I went to probably twenty doctors in Indiana and Kentucky getting x-rays, MRIs, and scans trying to find someone who could take out the plates. It wasn't until 2016 that I finally found a doctor who agreed to remove them. In the five years since then, I've been in pretty good shape and only have to go to the chiropractor once in a while to be worked on some.

As for my girls, Courtney got married in July 2020, which she remembers as being the fifth anniversary of when she first started dating this guy. He's a good guy and I like him—he believes in Jesus and is a Republican, so we get along pretty well. They got married in Las Vegas and then had their reception a few months later back here in Indiana. My ex, their mom, wasn't there either time. She was supposed to come and help Courtney pick out her wedding dress, but called about an hour ahead and said she couldn't make it. At least she called, right? In that respect, it's been a sad time for the girls. More than once I told them when they were younger that "You know, I may not be much, but I'm all you got."

As I write this, both Courtney and Grace are pregnant—Courtney is twenty-three and Grace is twenty-one—and I'm still there for them if and when they need me. Each of them has a company credit card from my company. I don't let them go crazy with it, but they can usually get something they want if they're needing it. When each of them found out they were expecting, they started talking about ordering this and ordering that. I told both of them, "Don't worry about buying anything you need for your kids. I want to go out and buy everything new that they need for each grandchild." They're like, "Really?" I'm like, "Yeah, I will give you the money and you use it to go buy whatever they need."

I'm blessed to be able to do that, and I'm going to get my grandchildren everything that I couldn't afford to get my daughters. I now have a successful business, and I might be able to pull this off, spoiling my grandkids. You know, business is good right now and, you know, I'm finally able to do what I couldn't do for them during those years of raising them. I guess I managed to do something right, despite all those stares I got from all those women working in schools and doctors' offices.

"I still go to him for a lot of my adult problems, asking things like, 'Well, what should I do about this situation? Do you think this is a good idea?'" Courtney said. "We've always been pretty honest to each other and open about anything. He's always been like, 'Well, you can always come to me with anything.' So I'm never second-guessing myself when I go to him with any problems I have or anything like that, which is always good.

"He still keeps a lot of his personal life to himself. He does come to me sometimes seeking my input on business decisions. Maybe he doesn't always listen, but he will ask."

Adds Grace, "He's a lot different now that we are both on our own than he was as a father, or when we were all under the same roof, because for us it was always about *surviving* and not necessarily *being*. Family life is about working; it's about being humble; it's about accepting what we can get, and being thankful for it.

"He did his best. He did his best," Grace added. "He was who God needed him to be and who I needed him to be. And we made it. I'm grown now and taking care of myself. Same thing for my sister. Do we have a thick skin? You've got to. All I worry about is me and my family. And I know that my father is always going to be who he is to me; he's going to be my rock at the end of the day.

"He still has things that he's going through or he's being challenged with, whether it's sobriety, things in his life or in his business, or even this book. That's fine; it doesn't affect me. He's in a place now to where I know he accepts things better. He's getting through them better and smarter and for himself and for the long run.

"One funny story I have about him is that every time we drive through the mountains in Tennessee, we listen to 'Mama Tried' by Merle Haggard. We both do this whether we're traveling together or one of us on our own. That's Mighty Merle right there. We laugh because we switch it up and always sing along saying 'Dad tried' instead. Hey, if we're at karaoke and you put in Merle Haggard, I will nail it. My dad raised me right getting me to listen to Merle Haggard, Johnny Cash, and all his other favorites."

9

This Is My Story and I'm Sticking to It

Once my daughters were fully grown and old enough to leave home on their own (but still attached at the heart to their old man), I ramped up my business, building it back to a full-time deal with some employees. That's where I'm at now. I'm back doing what I was doing before I raised two kids. We work pretty much nationwide or wherever the work takes us.

As of September 2020, during the worst part of the COVID-19 pandemic, I passed the thirty-year mark in the business of putting together and putting up communications towers. I still climb a little bit. But having passed the fifty-year mark in age, I'm getting too old to do that anymore on a regular basis. Younger guys on my crew are doing that for me now.

The business is located in Sullivan, Indiana. That's where I have my shop, and it's where I live with a travel trailer that I hitch behind my truck. I have the travel trailer hooked up to all the utility sources, and I stay in it when I'm in town, which isn't often.

Business is good. I'm making money and things are pretty

good. Because of the whole COVID-19 thing, I haven't been active in any church right now, although I consider myself both Protestant and Catholic, attending Mass in the evening when I can.

As far as speaking about my life, recovery, and hope, I haven't spoken at any churches or schools in a while, having decided to take a break from it for the time being. I've never advertised or promoted myself as some sort of speaker who gets paid, and I'm certainly no preacher or traveling evangelist. I've had collections taken up for me on occasion, but I never went into this with the idea of making money from it. Nor is anyone making me do it. I've never had any sort of speech training, coaching, or guidance on public speaking, but I speak from the heart and have a knack for tailoring my talk to whatever audience I happen to be standing in front of.

I must be doing something right and the message is apparently resonating because I have gotten asked many times to do this. I was planning to get back to it after I got this book done, maybe selling a few copies along the way, but more importantly touching the hearts and minds of people who perhaps can take something away from my story that is positive for them, as ugly as my story gets at times.

When I was first making my presentations at schools and churches, I would just focus on telling my testimony, how I had crashed and hit bottom before really embracing Jesus Christ as my Savior and rebuilding my life. In more recent years I have become more comfortable including my daughters in my talks, explaining how and why I got them out of their mother's custody, how we overcame things together as father and daughters, while segueing into my life recovery and rebuilding my life. I always know there is somebody in the room or the building who has had it as bad or worse than I and can perhaps glean something from my message that they can apply to their own lives. At least, that's my hope and prayer, in my own small way doing a piece of God's work in taking his message of salvation to a few small slices of this present world.

One thing I also have done in recent years, when speaking, is reveal more details about my life, the good, the bad, and the ugly, as they say. It's all about transparency. I like to talk about how I want to see my business be really successful and make my story come out really well, to have a truly, uplifting angle to it. I'm not quite to that point yet. I've made millions of dollars over the years, and almost all of that has gone right back out, but that's not the story. I still work every day just like anybody else.

One of the positives that has come out of my turbulent experiences, much of it self-inflicted, is an empathy and understanding that comes in handy for mentoring, sponsoring, and helping people with addictions. I have spoken at a lot of twelve-step meetings as well as at churches and schools. A couple of years ago, I acquired my CRS certification, which refers to a Certified Recovery Specialist. It's a state certification. Every state has it. People like me get this so they can work as certified counselors. I got it because I thought it would enhance my ability to help people. I spent a week of in-class training, which was ironic because I usually hate anything to do with classroom-type stuff—as my own past will attest to, going back to third grade. I don't use my CRS to get paid, but it's enhanced my ability to help people.

When I speak at a school, I try to find a connection with students at the start of my talk. When I started out doing this, I had a couple pastors and some school principals who didn't know me ask me to come talk to them first so they knew what I was going to say. All things considered, I prefer to speak at a church because I can say what I want to say. Schools, on the other hand, are caught up in this nonsense about separation of church and state that is meant to stifle Christians like me and put a limit on what we can say when speaking on school property. So I tiptoe around that as best I can. Over the years some school principals have told me to go ahead and talk about my Christianity, but I'm still reluctant to do that. All it takes is one person to object, and then it causes problems for the school, even if not for me. I like speaking at churches more because I like sharing my Christian testimony more than my alcoholic one. When I'm speaking at schools, my alcoholism and alcohol testimony are the main topics, but at church I can speak openly about how Christ has changed my life. Without telling that part of it, I'm leaving out the most important part of my story.

I spoke at a lot of places between 2009 at 2019, and I decided to take a break starting in 2020, in part to write this book. I went off of social media and have since been sort of hiding out—taking a break, actually. I needed to pause that part of my life because I was getting burned out talking about it. It is often cathartic talking about these often destructive but always instructive things in my life, but it can wear me down, too. I've lost track of the number of times I have told my story and testimony to people, when they are (usually) just hearing it for the first time. It gets old for me at times, probably because much of it is painful to relive. Even in my Christian walk, there's still so much shame in my life tugging at me. Usually, by the time I'm done sharing my testimony, I'm exhausted, even if it was for just twenty or thirty minutes. In those times I feel like I've been hit by a truck.

Part of the deal with me is that I've always been kind of backward and shy—not in terms of intelligence or in standing up for myself, but in my not being the sort of fellow who has a strong, engaging personality. I'm more of the silent, dark stranger sort of dude, often more at home in the shadows than in the spotlight. I still have to force myself to get up there to speak onstage, like at a church, but once I get up there a calm comes over me. At least I've never turned around and run off yet.

The first time I was asked to speak was at a halfway house about a half-hour from where I lived—it was a halfway house for recovering drug addicts and alcoholics. They had twelve-step meetings there, such as AA, and some were speaker meetings during which someone comes up and shares his or her testimony. I had never done that. Although I had been sober for six years, I had never shared my story in front of others. That first talk was pretty short; I hadn't thought about it much. I just did it off the top of my head, unrehearsed—no problem, I had lived it. Within the next year, I was being asked to speak at schools, and things just snowballed from there.

As much as I was speaking, maybe once or twice a month on average, I don't think I was on social media at the time and certainly wasn't advertising myself as a speaker. I wasn't getting paid and didn't expect to—that's not what I'm about. What happened to get all this started was that I was playing on a church league softball team and at the ballfield met a woman who was a health teacher at the school. We got to talking, just a friendly chat between games. The church I had been going to was a fairly large church, with about five hundred people in the congregation. I knew a lot of people and they knew me, but they didn't know my testimony. How could they? I had never given it in public.

I told this woman a brief version of my story, and she immediately asked me if I would come speak to her class. That turned into a fairly regular gig—each semester she would have a different set of students in her class, and these students wouldn't know about my story until they heard me give one of my presentations. I would give two presentations a year—one for each of two semesters for nine years, through 2019. Word got around and soon another school asked me to come speak, and that's what I did.

After that I spoke at a lot of different places, such as at a Tres Dias weekend for Protestants as well as a Cursillo for a Catholic church. I even got a standing ovation at one point. I've also been involved with a prison ministry over the years. If they want me to speak, I definitely have something to say.

I was a little bit nervous when it came to the prison. I had done some volunteer work there, helping out with AA meetings. People in church got me involved in this. It involved five Saturdays of training, eight hours a day—a total of forty hours—focusing on such things as what to say and what not to say. What makes you nervous going into a prison to speak is that you end up talking to a lot of people who have made a lot of mistakes, some of them pretty bad. Still, a lot of them are good people who have made bad choices. That includes me, but by the grace of God I have never been incarcerated.

When I go into those prisons, it's to (hopefully) bring them to Christ and how they can be shown forgiveness. It involves two weekends a year, and I've been to seven of these over the last twelve years. An interesting side note, though: There I was, thinking I would show and tell them all about those good things like forgiveness and salvation. And it ended up just as much the other way around, as I found out that by helping them I was able to forgive myself for my past. I discovered how much anger and resentment I had toward myself and others.

A lot of emotional things go on during those weekends. I remember my first Sunday at one of those prison events, walking outside on a gorgeous autumn October day and being hit with so many emotions, tears running down my cheeks. I thought to myself, *I'm different!* I wasn't sure how I was different, but I knew my life had been changed. Even though I had been sober for six years at this point, for the first time I finally felt that I was free, that I was on the road to recovery. I found a place I belonged, a group of men—fellow team members, about forty or fifty of us—we had a lot in common. Almost all of the other guys there were old enough to be my dad, with me being one of the youngest. Even after I turned fifty, I was still one of the youngest, as most of these other guys were between about sixty and maybe eighty-five and retired.

Some of what I talk about to these groups is difficult to discuss. The hardest part is going back over the time I hit rock bottom and tried to take my life at age thirty-three—not that long ago when you think about it, less than twenty years. I get pretty emotional when I get to that point—every time I speak—and always have to pause for a bit. I also get emotional talking about my daughters and what they have had to go through, especially with their mother's situation and our divorce and custody battle and all that went on with that for several years. I talk about the battles we had to fight over the years, and which my daughters still have to fight to this day.

I close this out by letting my daughters carry this story across the finish line, recalling those times when they have attended one of these events at which I have spoken.

"It's sometimes been kind of hard to take it in because I don't have any memories of him beforehand," my older daughter, Courtney, said for this book. "Like, I don't really remember how bad it was before he got sober. But it's definitely good that he gets his message out there in such a way that other people can relate to. He's always said, 'Even if what I say helps just one person, it's worthwhile getting out there and speaking.'

"You can tell he gets a little antsy about it at times, though. That's when he sometimes hurries himself a little bit too much and forgets to stop and breathe. I'm pretty bad about that myself."

"I've gone to different schools and churches with my dad to hear him speak," Grace said. "When I've gone with him, I've just sat there and prayed and hoped that however God led him there to speak, he would get through to those listening. I believe that he's up there doing what he's supposed to be doing, because if God called him to be there and do this, then I will support him.

"It's been odd at times how people hearing him will then say to me, 'Omigosh! That's what happened? That's your dad? That's not the same man that I know.' And I will tell them, 'What you're hearing is just the bottom line, but that's not the whole ordeal.'"